(U

MW00994770

AMAZON.COM)

Larry Thompson

(814) 873-6696

NATURE, GOD, AND PULPIT

Nature, God, and Pulpit

Elizabeth Achtemeier

William B. Eerdmans Publishing Company
Grand Rapids, Michigan

255 Jefferson Ave. S.E., Grand Rapids, Mich. 49503

Printed in the United States of America

Library of Congress Cataloging-in-Publication Data

Achtemeier, Elizabeth Rice, 1926-
Nature, God, pulpit / Elizabeth Achtemeier.
p. cm.
Includes indexes.
ISBN 0-8028-3706-9 (hard)
1. Creation — Biblical teaching. 2. Nature — Biblical teaching.
3. God — Biblical teaching. 4. Preaching. 5. Sermons, American.
6. Meditations. I. Title.
BS680.C69A35 1992
231.7 — dc20 92-24693
CIP

Contents

Preface

This book is intended to draw together and to interpret for the church's preachers, in a clear and reasonably comprehensive fashion, the biblical materials having to do with the natural world and God's relation to it. It is a project that needs to be done, I believe, because few subjects have been more neglected by the pulpit in this country in recent years than an explication of the relation between nature and God.

Moreover, preachers are not being offered many resources to overcome such neglect. There are increasing numbers of books being published that deal with the relation of science and religion, as a glance at the notes in this volume will show. But many of those books are rather scientifically technical and difficult for preachers with a limited amount of time to devote to them. Further, a number of denominations have issued study papers dealing with the ecological crisis and the church's responsibility toward it, but these have not dealt in a comprehensive way with the biblical materials about nature. Thus, this volume is an attempt to present the biblical witness concerning God and the natural world in a way that will furnish preachers with content for sermons on the subject.

Chapters 1 through 6 of this book were first presented as the

Payton Lectures of 1992 at Fuller Theological Seminary in Pasadena, California, and I wish to thank the administration, faculty, and students of Fuller for their many kindnesses and for the opportunity of sharing and discussing this material with them.

I also wish to thank our son, P. Mark Achtemeier, who took time out from his Ph.D. studies in theology and science to read through my manuscript, to make theological suggestions, and to correct some of my explanations of scientific theory. Any remaining inaccuracies are mine and not his. But to him, and to my beloved husband, children, children-in-law, and grandchildren, this book is dedicated.

Richmond, Virginia
1992

ELIZABETH ACHTEMEIER

CHAPTER 1

Not Far Enough

Certainly the Christian church in the United States has a fully developed doctrine of redemption, and it is that message of redemption which is heard from most pulpits in most churches on most Sunday mornings — that we are all sinners, that Jesus Christ died for our sins, that we have been redeemed from sin and death by his cross and resurrection, and that by the power of the Holy Spirit, we can live a new life in a new community, under the lordship of Christ. That message forms the heart of our Christian proclamation, and happily, there are now few regular churchgoers who are not aware of that glad good news.

The difficulty, however, is that our preaching and teaching of redemption in Jesus Christ have not gone far enough. In the Bible, faith in the redemption wrought by God issues in particular understandings of the creation and of God's relation to it, and our modern-day churches rarely push on to examine those understandings.

Indeed, we do not even have a commonly accepted theological name for such understandings. One could say that they are all encompassed in the doctrine of creation, but the average churchgoer would take that to mean a doctrine of how the world began, and that is only one part of the Bible's understanding of the universe. The biblical writers have a comprehensive view of the cosmos and of God's relation to it, not only in its beginning but as it continues and as it will end, and it is that comprehensive view which we have neglected.

There are many reasons for such neglect. Certainly our migration from rural to urban settings has created a distance between us and the natural world. Farmers must adjust to the rhythms of "seedtime and harvest, cold and heat, summer and winter, day and night," but urban dwellers can largely ignore them all in the artificial settings of fluorescent lights and air conditioning, heat pumps and greenhouses, workweeks and holidays. There are thousands of people in our cities who have never seen a cow, and who could not say if the stars were out because city lights and smog block their vision. A youth leader in New York City took his teenage group into the country and found, to his amazement, that they were terrified when they saw a deer. The natural world has become strange to us, divorced from our thoughts and vocabulary, so that few sermons anymore even use natural images — a development that has impoverished our language almost beyond imagination. As George Buttrick remarked at the beginning of the space age, "We admire Sputnik and ignore the stars." It is now our own creations that capture our attention instead. Our animals are anthropomorphized into Mickey Mouse and Snoopy. Tiny transistors are more amazing to us than seeds. Concentrating only on our manufactured things, we have lost the natural world.

Certainly too we have not preached and taught a biblical, cosmological theology because modern science has replaced so much of our former religious approach to the natural world. Despite the astounding advances in modern physics and astrology, most people still view the world from the standpoint of Newtonian physics, thinking largely in terms of natural causality. Therefore, in times past, that which we could not explain in nature's realm we attributed to the supernatural — to a so-called "God-of-the-gaps," who became the cause of the marvelous and inexplicable. But science, in its unceasing quest to understand reality, has explained more and more, and to the layperson's mind, few gaps in our knowledge remain anymore, and there is left no place in the cosmos for God to work. All happens by natural cause and proceeds according to natural law. And though most churchgoers still believe that God created the world, they also believe that he has little relation to its workings. The cosmos is for them a secular realm in which the divine has no ongoing part, and the only ones who can explain our universe for us are our scientists, who, in contrast to the faith we place in them, are speaking more and more in terms of mystery.

To be sure, it is good that we got rid of the God-of-the-gaps, and our scientists have made wonderful contributions both to our knowledge and to our well-being. Let no one think that the Christian faith has to battle against modern-day scientific progress. The days when the church could condemn a Galileo should be far in the past. Nevertheless, the Christian faith must recover its biblical, cosmological theology if it is going to minister to our age.

There is a great hunger abroad in the land for some reconnection with the natural realm. Urban dwellers spill out of the eastern megapolis to visit the Amish country, with its horse-drawn buggies and rejection of electricity. Church groups take off for retreats in the woods, and apartment dwellers buy Gro-lights. People make household companions of parrots and ferrets, of reptiles and even skunks and Chinese pigs. Petting zoos swarm with kids, and lakefront lots sell for thousands. There is something deep in our being which makes us know that Adam (*'adam* in the Hebrew) was created from the *'adamah* (the ground), and we long for a reconciliation with the natural world we have lost.

And yet, there is a kind of emptiness to it all. As Helmut Thielicke has written,

> Is it really joy in the beauty of the world that drives us through the country at sixty or seventy miles an hour, that disgorges troops of tourists from their buses in the great and famous spots only to be sucked up again — after sending off a few hundred post-

> cards — as with a vacuum sweeper? And a hundred yards away from these fat pastures of the travel industry, a hundred yards from the scenic competition of popular resorts, there where the crickets sing, nobody is to be found.[1]

We hunger for the natural realm, but we do not know how to be reconnected with it, and that is partly the fault of the Christian church, which has not preached and taught a whole theology.

The result is that a number of alien faiths are rushing in to fill the void, like those seven evil spirits in the Gospel according to Matthew, who find an empty place in a man and rush in to occupy its space. Some are telling us, for example, that we will truly appreciate and understand the natural world if we adopt the animism of early American Indians,[2] while the New Age religionists wish us to see it in terms of a Hindu-like monism. Similarly, some feminist theologians want us to believe that the world is the body of God and that panentheism is the true faith, or that the pantheism of the ancients is the only proper religion. Other writers

1. Thielicke, *How the World Began: Man in the First Chapters of the Bible,* translated and with an introduction by John W. Doberstein (Philadelphia: Muhlenberg Press, 1961), p. 29.

2. At the 1991 World Council of Churches meeting in Canberra, Australia, which had the theme "Come, Holy Spirit, Renew the Whole Creation," some participants suggested that the aborigines of Australia could teach an approach to the creation better than that of Christianity: "The suggestion is that the complicity of the churches in environmental degradation and exploitation, and the central source of such practices in the doctrines of human dominion and stewardship, require new theological directions. 'The earth is crying out' according to a WCC pre-Assembly document, and we therefore must explore what is wrong with our theology of creation. Those who are closest to the land, and *whose spiritualities consider the earth to be sacred* [emphasis mine], are those best able to guide this new process. It is to be regretted, therefore, not only that such evil was done to aboriginal people, but that their very spirituality was violated by the introduction of Christianity in Australia" (reported by Lawrence E. Adams, "The WCC at Canberra: Which Spirit?" *First Things: A Monthly Journal of Religion and Public Life,* no. 14, June/July 1991, p. 30). This is the same argument often used in relation to North American Indians. At its base are gross misunderstandings of the relation of God to the natural world.

urge us to see the divine in the natural processes of the world, while some believe that the nature of God must be deduced from the findings of modern physics. All such positions are foreign to the biblical faith, and there is no possibility of living an abundant life in our universe on the basis of such distortions. But we can overcome the distortions only if we know what biblical, cosmological theology teaches.

Certainly too the ecological crisis of our time has emphasized for us the urgency of reclaiming the whole of the biblical faith. There is no doubt that we are slowly destroying the natural world. Numbers of endangered species of plants and animals become extinct every day. Fertile land is covered over with asphalt parking lots and shopping centers. Wetlands fall victim to summer home development. The Chesapeake Bay's oysters disappear. The earth's oxygen is depleted by the felling of thousands of acres of rain forest, its ozone layer pockmarked by the spray of chlorofluorocarbons. Aquifers are dried up by overuse and overpopulation. And the clean, shining structures of the future that we see imagined on *Star Trek* present to us an antiseptic world devoid of green and growth.

But as Joseph Sittler has written, "Man's selfhood hangs upon the persistence of the earth,"[3] and for all our technology, we cannot live apart from nature's bounty. It is no accident, in Genesis 1, that human beings were created after the sun and moon, and after the plants and animals and fishes. Indeed, Loren Eiseley once wrote that human beings were not possible until flowering plants with their seeds appeared.[4]

We can hoard the gifts of the natural realm or misuse them or use them up. Worse still, we can render them all sterile by detonating a few hydrogen bombs. Knowing how to live with nature is a matter of our life or death.

Yet, finally it is not the ecological crisis or the fear of atomic

3. Sittler, *The Care of the Earth and Other University Sermons*, ed. Edmund Steimle, Preacher's Paperback Library (Philadelphia: Fortress Press, 1964), p. 89.

4. Eiseley, *The Immense Journey* (New York: Random House–Vintage Books, 1946), pp. 63-66.

destruction that should drive us to teach and preach a whole theology in the church and outside of it. Some writers, such as Sallie McFague, have implied that such fear is the reason for a theology of the cosmos.[5] But our Lord warned us against all views concerned primarily with our physical well-being: "Do not fear those who kill the body but cannot kill the soul," he said. "Rather fear him who can destroy both soul and body in hell" (Matt. 10:28) — namely, God. And surely that is part of the message too of Job and of psalms such as Psalm 73. We have finally to do with God in our lives, and he is the one upon whom we are dependent for our *eternal* life or death. Isaiah 2:6-22 and Jeremiah 4:23-26 picture a far worse fate than that connected with atomic destruction — the universe subjected to the wrath of the God who made all things and who can unmake them.

We have first to do with God. And we cannot properly understand ourselves or the universe apart from him, nor can we live in our world as we were meant to live until we begin to understand God's relation with all he has made.

It is that understanding of God's relation to his creation which we seek in this book, in the hope that it will aid the church to teach and to preach a whole biblical theology.

5. McFague, *Models of God: Theology for an Ecological, Nuclear Age* (Philadelphia: Fortress Press, 1987). See also her essay entitled "An Earthly Theological Agenda," in *How My Mind Has Changed*, ed. James M. Wall and David Heim (Grand Rapids: William B. Eerdmans, 1991). McFague is right when she says that theology must concern all of creation. But her theology misinterprets both the nature of human beings, whom she sees only as "earthlings" and not in any sense as "aliens" on the planet, and the nature of God. God is, she writes, "immanently present in the processes of the universe, including those of our planet" ("An Earthly Theological Agenda," p. 140). Thus she has written that the world is the "body of God."

CHAPTER 2

How Do We Know?

Before we can say anything about the Bible's understanding of the natural world and of God's relation to it, we must first make clear the source and the nature of our knowledge.

Some Forms of Natural Religion

Certainly all other religions in the world except the Judeo-Christian faith (imitated by Islam) are based on natural theology; that is, they start with the world and deduce the nature of God from the world's phenomena. Indeed, the peoples surrounding Israel in biblical times identified their gods with natural forces and happenings. Not only the Babylonians and Egyptians but also the Greeks and Romans saw in the manifestations of nature the life and activity of the divine. The expanse of the sky, the heat of the sun, the growth and death of vegetation, the fury of the storm — these were to those ancient peoples not impersonal happenings and objects but cosmic thous that affected human life and demanded adjustment to them. Nature was alive for early peoples. Its conflicts were the struggles of opposing gods, as in Greek mythology. Its harmony was the result of the organization of the cosmic state by the gods, as in Mesopotamian theology. Or its harmony stemmed from the genealogical relationships of the gods, as in Hesiod's *Theogony*.

In short, the natural world, with all its life forces, was identified with the divine, and the aim of worship then became to identify with the gods and goddesses of nature and to influence them through the rituals of the cult. In the Canaan in which biblical Israel lived, for example, Baal was the god of fertility, and the practice of sacred prostitution in the cult was designed to influence Baal, through sympathetic magic, to bring forth fertility in the natural realm.

Such identification of the divine with nature is the oldest religion in the world, and it is the most persistent, found in every culture from the most primitive to the most sophisticated. Some Hindus still worship monkeys or sacred cows, just as some modern American church groups retreat to rustic settings to "be closer to God." A contemporary homiletics professor once prayed, "Teach us, O infinite God, to see Thee in all creation — in the stars as well as in the daisies." And Starhawk, a well-known feminist author, has written this about her deity called the Mother Goddess:

> The Goddess is . . . earth — Mother Earth, who sustains all growing things, who is the body, our bones and cells. She is air . . . fire . . . water . . . mare, cow, cat, owl, crane, flower, tree, apple, seed, lion, sow, stone, woman. She is found in the world around us, in the cycles and seasons of nature, and in mind, body, spirit, and the emotions within each of us. Thou art Goddess. I am Goddess. All that lives . . . all that serves life, is Goddess.[1]

This identification of the divine with the natural world was nourished in the closing decades of the eighteenth century by the

1. Starhawk, "Witchcraft and Women's Culture," in *Womanspirit Rising: A Feminist Reader in Religion*, ed. Carol P. Christ and Judith Plaskow (San Francisco: Harper & Row, 1979), p. 263.

poetic voices of Wordsworth and the other Romantics. It was also fostered by Francis Bacon, who, in accord with earlier thinkers, insisted in the seventeenth century that nature was a source of revelation equal to that of the Bible[2] and who thus laid the philosophical foundation for the Deism of the eighteenth century, which insisted that the existence and attributes of God were clearly and unambiguously revealed in his handiwork and that any further revelation was superfluous, "particularly one so obscure and contradictory as the Biblical revelation."[3]

Such natural religion takes many forms, from the sophisticated reasoning of Paul Tillich and J. A. T. Robinson, who identify God with the Ground of Being in, through, and under all things, to the simplistic worship of the layperson who finds God revealed in the beauty of lakes and trees. Most recently, its principal champions have been many of our New Age and feminist theologians. Consider this passage from radical feminist Carol Christ, who finds the holy identified with the goddess of a Greek cave in a cliff in the sea at Eressos:

> She appears to me while I am floating in the embrace of the azure sea, rising up from the water in the shape of an enormous vagina. . . . Watching the water flow in and out of her, I feel drawn to her center. I climb up and lean back into the crevice. As my body relaxes, I feel a surge of energy, the life force flowing through me. My rhythms merge with hers, the shapes of the rock become the shapes of my body pulsating with energy, flowing into the sea. . . . Near the cave is a tiny church which is dedicated to . . . Mary. . . . [But] I know which place for me is All Holy.[4]

Similarly, Rosemary Ruether has written, we "reclaim our true relationship with somatic reality, with body and earth, and with

2. As noted in the discussion by George S. Hendry in *Theology of Nature* (Philadelphia: Westminster Press, 1980), pp. 55-56.

3. Ibid., p. 57.

4. Christ, *Laughter of Aphrodite: Reflections on a Journey to the Goddess* (San Francisco: Harper & Row, 1987), p. 226.

the Great Goddess that sustains our life in nature."[5] Thus is the divine identified with the creation, and the nature of the divine is then deduced from the phenomena of the universe.

The Biblical View

Many persons, of course, have tried to find such natural religion in the Bible. When they read Psalm 8, for example, they believe that the Psalmist knows God from looking at the heavens:

> When I look at your heavens, the work of your fingers,
> the moon and the stars that you have established;
> what are human beings that you are mindful of them,
> mortals that you care for them?
>
> (vv. 3-4, NRSV)

Or they see Psalm 19 as portraying the revelation of God through nature:

> The heavens are telling the glory of God;
> and the firmament proclaims his handiwork.
>
> (v. 1)

Or they point to Psalm 29, in which thunder is the "voice of the Lord," or to Psalm 104, or to the soaring hymns of Second Isaiah, or to the speech of God in Job, chapters 38–41. And Romans 1 is used to clinch the argument: "Ever since the creation of the world [God's] eternal power and divine nature, invisible though they are, have been understood and seen through the things he has made. So [the Gentiles] are without excuse; for though they knew God, they did not honor him" (vv. 20-21, NRSV).

In regard to the Old Testament, there can be no doubt that the created world suggested something of God to the Hebrew

5. Ruether, *Women-Church* (San Francisco: Harper & Row, 1986), p. 108.

mind. Certainly the author of Psalm 104 found reflected in the harmony of the world the wisdom and faithfulness of its Creator, just as for the author of Psalm 29, a thunderstorm rising out of the north over the Mediterranean manifested the power of God in nature's rage. God's speech to Job, in chapters 38–41, tells of the mystery and care of God that the wonders of creation show, just as the same mystery of the Creator God's love is borne in upon the writer of Psalm 8 by the inspiring sight of the heavens. Every people, in every age, has been awestruck by the order, the mystery, and the power in nature that seem to point to something beyond them.

But the Hebrews did not know their God by finding him first in nature. They knew him because they had first been found by him, and the God they saw behind nature's wonders was the God they knew first from history. For example, the praise we find in Psalm 8 is not the result of knowing God in the heavens but has its source in the same theology that is found in Genesis 1, and that Psalmist knew his God from that received creation tradition handed down to him in the cult. Psalm 29 may identify God's voice with the thunder, but the climax of its praise is the affirmation by God's historical people in the temple on Zion that God has entered into covenant with them as their King (vv. 10-11). While Psalm 19 hears the heavens telling the glory of God, it goes on to affirm that it is God's revealed law which revives the soul and enlightens the eyes (vv. 7-8). The Creator God of Second Isaiah is above all the Redeemer who shapes history to come (44:6-8), who stirs up Cyrus of Persia to release God's people in a new exodus (43:14-21; 45:12-13), who calls his servant Israel to be a light and covenant to the nations (42:5-7). Wherever there is found in the Old Testament the revelation of God in nature, it is accompanied by the revelation of God in Israel's history. Indeed, in the one or two instances in which this is not true, in which there is no recital of the Lord's acts in history, it can be shown that Israel has borrowed from its pagan environment and that such exceptions should be understood in the context of the Old Testament as a whole, as, for example, with Psalm 104, which may be based upon the Egyptian hymn to the creator god Aton.

Had Israel not first known God from their history with him, they never would have recognized him truly in the natural world, a statement that can best be illustrated by the Kenites in the book of Exodus. Apparently, according to Exodus, the Kenites, a tribe of Midian in the Sinai peninsula, knew the name of Yahweh, but apparently too they worshiped him as a God of a sacred mountain or as a storm god. And the Kenites differed little from other nomadic tribes of the ancient Near East. They produced no prophets and no sacred history. They had no sense of a special mission in the world. They never would have claimed that Yahweh controlled the universe, much less that he was directing it toward a goal. Yahweh was known to them only in nature, and their knowledge of their God was limited by that means of revelation. It was only when Yahweh took the decisive step of revealing himself through the concrete events of history that the full magnitude and glory of his purpose and person became known. It was only when Yahweh delivered Israel at the Sea of Reeds out of slavery into freedom and confronted Israel through Moses at Sinai that Jethro the Kenite, the priest of Midian, could confess, "Now I know that the Lord is greater than all gods, because he delivered the people from under the hand of the Egyptians" (Exod. 18:11).

Indeed, the Old Testament goes to great lengths to ensure that Israel does not identify its God with the creation he has made. As is well known, Genesis 1 employs some of the language of the *Enuma elish,* the Babylonian creation myth, as do Psalms 89:9-10 and 74:12-14 and Isaiah 51:9. In that myth, the god of Babylon, Marduk, fights against the goddess of chaos, Tiamat, slays her, cuts her body in two, and lifts up half of it to form the firmament, while the other half forms the earth beneath. "Tiamat" may be the linguistic equivalent of *tehom* ("deep") in Genesis 1:2, and the picture of God creating the firmament in the midst of the chaotic waters, in Genesis 1:6, and then lifting it up to form the arc of the sky, in Genesis 1:7, echoes the Babylonian picture. In fact, very often where one finds references to the "dragon" or "Leviathan" or "Rahab" or the "sea" in the Old Testament, there is an echo of the language of the Babylonian chaos dragon myth, and the reference is to the primeval waters of chaos (e.g., in Ps. 46:1-3).

However, while the Old Testament writers borrow the language of their time, they have completely demythologized it. In the Babylonian myth, the gods emanate out of the chaotic waters; in Genesis and elsewhere, God's Spirit is above the chaos, and he is Lord over it. In the myth, the fight between Tiamat and Marduk takes place in the timeless realm of the gods; in Genesis, the creation is the first act in time. In the myth, Marduk has to struggle with Tiamat; in Genesis, God merely speaks and creation is accomplished. Indeed, the only connection between God and his creation, according to Genesis 1, is his sovereign Word. Throughout the Bible, God works with the world through the agency of his Word or of his Spirit, a fact which John 1 then affirms when it says that "in the beginning was the Word . . . and . . . all things were made through him, and without him was not anything made that was made." The Bible never identifies that Word, which is Jesus Christ, or his Spirit with the created world. "He who comes from above is above all," Jesus says. "He who is of the earth belongs to the earth" (John 3:31); "You are from below, I am from above; you are of this world, I am not of this world" (John 8:23).

The Old Testament is therefore very clear about the fact that God lived before all creation:

> Lord, you have been our dwelling place
>   in all generations.
> Before the mountains were brought forth,
>   or ever you had formed the earth and the world,
>   from everlasting to everlasting you are God.
>
> (Ps. 90:1-2, NRSV)

The Old Testament also knows that God endures, though heaven and earth pass away:

Long ago you laid the foundation of the earth,
and the heavens are the work of your hands.
They will perish, but you endure;
they will all wear out like a garment.
You change them like clothing, and they pass away;
but you are the same, and your years have no end.
(Ps. 102:25-27, NRSV)[6]

The God of Israel cannot be identified with the cosmos that he has created, and that cosmos is therefore inadequate to reveal the true nature of God (cf. Ps. 76:4).

What, then, of Paul's statement in Romans 1:20-21 that God's "eternal power and divine nature" have been "seen through the things he has made"? Paul's answer would be that sin has corrupted our vision, as it has corrupted all of creation itself (Rom. 8:22; 1 Cor. 2:6-16; Acts 17:22-31), and this is the message handed on by John Calvin also:

> Bright, however, as is the manifestation which God gives both of himself and [of] his immortal kingdom in the mirror of his works, so great is our stupidity, so dull are we in regard to these bright manifestations, that we derive no benefit from them.[7]

> When Paul says that that which may be known of God is manifested by the creation of the world, he does not mean such a manifestation as may be comprehended by the wit of man (Rom. i.19); on the contrary, he shows that it has no further effect than to render us inexcusable (Acts xvii.27).[8]

"Now we see in a mirror dimly" (1 Cor. 13:12), and the true nature of God cannot be known through the revelation of himself in what he has made.

6. Cf. Isa. 51:6; 54:10; Mark 13:31 and parallels.

7. Calvin, *Institutes of the Christian Religion,* trans. Henry Beveridge (1949; reprint Grand Rapids: William B. Eerdmans, 1972), 1.5.11.

8. Ibid., 1.5.14.

I think this is borne in upon me every time I sit at night on the screened-in porch of the summer cabin my husband built for us in the woods of the Pocono Mountains. One can hear the struggle of nature going on in the dark of that surrounding forest — the squeal of a chipmunk caught in the jaws of a black snake, the frantic chirps of a mother bird whose eggs are being stolen by a raccoon, even the splash of a fish that leaps above the surface of the lake to catch a passing bug. If nature is revelatory of our God, then it reveals a purpose of death as well as of life, and the lesson we must draw is that the big gods eat the little gods.

The God of the Bible is not revealed through the universe that he has made because he is not identified with the universe, and therefore nothing in the natural world is adequate to reveal his nature. Every people senses something of mystery, of power, of wisdom from the creation around them. But that creation cannot reveal that God is a God of forgiveness whose goal is to make himself a people. It cannot reveal that he desires above all else to live in fellowship with that people. It cannot reveal his sacrifice of his only Son to found that fellowship. The God of the Bible makes his true nature known not in his works in nature but through his works and words in history, and it was the revelation of God to Israel in history that led to her confession of God's lordship over nature.

The Basis of Israel's Confession

Why then did Israel confess, in Genesis 1, that the Lord brought order out of chaos by his creative Word? She made that confession of faith because not just once but time and again in her history she had known God's power to conquer life's chaos with his Word and to create a future where none had seemed possible (cf. Rom. 4:17). Throughout her life, Israel was confronted with a God who had the power to thwart the empire of Egypt and to turn back the army of the Assyrians, who had the might to roll back the Sea of

Reeds or to punish his disobedient people with drought (1 Kings 17–18; Amos 4:7-8; Jer. 14:1-10), who had the sovereignty to kill (2 Kings 1:17; Jer. 28:16-17; Deut. 32:39; 1 Sam. 2:6; cf. 5:1-12) and to make alive (1 Kings 17:21-22; 2 Kings 4:29-37; Isa. 38:5; cf. James 4:12; Rev. 1:17-18). Israel therefore confessed that such a God had ultimate power in his hands, that he alone could call the universe into being and sustain its life, that he alone was sovereign Lord and Creator of the visible world. Israel's confession of God as "the Maker of heaven and earth," a phrase that is found throughout the Bible, was derived from her experience of God in history, and apart from that sacred history, Israel never would have known God truly.

We might say that, according to the Bible, the revelation of God in his universe is like those highway reflectors that we see along our roadways. They give no light in themselves. But if we shine our car headlights on them, they shine back at us. So it is too with God's revelation in the natural world. In and of itself, nature gives no true knowledge of God. But if you shine the light of God's revelation of himself in history on the universe, then indeed it does give back knowledge of God. Then trees and mountains, birds and fish sing out, "The hand that made us is divine." Then the heavens in fact tell the glory of God, and the firmament proclaims his handiwork. Then the beauty, the order, the fertility, the life that surround us become wonderful gifts, and we can exult, as Israel exulted, in God's care for his creation:

> Thou crownest the year with thy bounty;
> the tracks of thy chariot drip with fatness.
> The pastures of the wilderness drip,
> the hills gird themselves with joy,
> the meadows clothe themselves with flocks,
> the valleys deck themselves with grain,
> they shout and sing together for joy.
>
> (Ps. 65:11-13)

On the one hand, the natural world was taken away from Israel. She could no longer worship it, as the people surrounding her worshiped it and as so many are worshiping it today. But on the other hand, nature was given back to Israel with a glory far exceeding that known in any natural religion. It was given back as the loving gift of the God of redemption. It is for this reason that Joseph Sittler could write, "My theology is not one derived from nature; it is a theology of the incarnation applied to nature — which is quite different."[9] The doctrine of the natural world, for the church, is derived from the doctrine of redemption, and we must understand Exodus 14 before we can understand Genesis 1.

Implications for the Church

This means for the church that unless we somehow participate in that sacred history which is now handed down to us in the Scriptures, unless the story of redemption becomes the story of our lives also, we cannot make the confession "I believe in God the Father Almighty, Maker of heaven and earth." It is no accident in the Apostles' Creed that it goes on to confess the history of Jesus Christ, "born of the virgin Mary; suffered under Pontius Pilate; was crucified, dead, and buried; he descended into hell; the third day he rose again from the dead; he ascended into heaven, and sitteth at the right hand of God the Father." Only if the story of redemption is told is there basis for belief in the Maker of heaven and earth, and that redemption must be the story of our redemption if we are to know God truly in relation to his universe. As Calvin wrote,

> It being thus manifest that God, foreseeing the inefficiency of his image imprinted on the fair form of the universe, has given the

9. Sittler, *Gravity and Grace: Reflections and Provocations,* ed. Linda Marie Delloff (Minneapolis: Augsburg Publishing House, 1986), p. 67.

> assistance of his Word to all whom he has ever been pleased to instruct effectually, we, too, must pursue this straight path, if we aspire in earnest to a genuine contemplation of God.[10]

In short, the church must preach and teach the Scriptures, with their whole history of redemption from Genesis to Revelation, if it wants its people to understand the true nature of God. There is no shortcut to the God of the Bible, no perception of his true character and will from the universe around us, no consciousness-raising that will reveal him to us, no discovery of some Ground of Being in the depths of all things apart from the sacred history. Only the God who saves is the God who creates and sustains (Ps. 121:2).

But then the church must go on from its teaching and preaching of redemption to the implications of those for the material universe. A hundred different voices are telling us these days what the relationship is between the divine and the world of nature — and so many of the voices are wrong, because they have not seen the world in the light of the historical revelation of its Maker. "Basically, it's quite simple," writes Helmut Thielicke. "If the world is the work of God, then it is clear that I can understand this work only by starting with its author."[11] And we can start with its Author only from his historical revelation of himself, given us through his people Israel and supremely in Jesus Christ.

Could it be that our distorted relation with the natural world and our ecological crisis are due to the fact that we no longer truly know nature's Lord? Certainly that was true in Israel. Israel turned to the worship of Baal, says the Lord, because

> . . . she did not know
> that it was I who gave her
> the grain, the wine, and the oil,

10. Calvin, *Institutes*, 1.6.3.

11. Thielicke, *I Believe: The Christian's Creed*, trans. John W. Doberstein and H. George Anderson (Philadelphia: Fortress Press, 1968), p. 37.

and who lavished upon her silver
and gold which they used for Baal.

(Hos. 2:8)

If we do not truly know nature's Lord, we end up, as Paul says, worshiping the creation rather than the Creator (Rom. 1:25). And if we do not know God's true relation to nature, then we start to believe that we are gods and can do with the natural world what we like. Listen once again to Thielicke:

> If someone bases his life simply on the creation and does not know the Creator himself but knows only Nature and her laws, he obviously cannot avoid exploiting all the possibilities with which Nature is endowed. He will develop a great Promethean passion to mobilize the entire physical and biological potential of Nature. He will want not only to learn about all her slumbering powers, but also to utilize them for technical purposes and make them subservient to his will. Man as the Lord of nature and the manager of her powers; man as the great director of natural laws; man as the goal of all things — that will become his pride and his passion. His dream is to have everything in the world be "possible" and to have all the world at his disposal.[12]

"Nothing that they propose to do will now be impossible for them" (Gen. 11:6). Such was the promethean temptation at the Tower of Babel, and we still see that temptation laid before us by the technology of our age, which has learned how to manipulate atoms and DNA genetic codes and the life cycles of all living things.

It is absolutely necessary that we truly know God and his relation to his universe. But as persons of faith have always confessed, we can know him only through his Word — the witness to his speech and action in history — illumined for us by his Spirit.

12. Ibid., p. 38.

CHAPTER 3

The Reserved Room

In Genesis 26:17-22, there is a little story about Isaac's attempt to settle in the valley of Gerar in Palestine, at the southern end of the Philistine Plain. After repeated disputes over well water with the herdsmen in the area, Isaac finally gains a well of his own and is left in peace, whereupon he exclaims, "Now the Lord has made room for us, and we shall be fruitful in the land" (v. 22). His statement, out of context, might be used by us, and indeed by all living things on this planet, as an affirmation of God's grace in creating the world. "The Lord has made room for us."

The Wonders of the Room

From the standpoint of modern science, there are currently two principal theories concerning the origin and existence of the universe. The first is that the universe had its beginning in an enormous explosion of densely concentrated matter, which was dispersed by the explosion to form the galaxies — the "big bang theory." A variation of this theory is that of an "oscillating universe" in which there is a state of alternating expansion and contraction. The second theory posits that the universe has always existed and will always exist by virtue of a continuous creation of new matter — the "steady state theory." Apparently, the measurement of the spectrum of light rays from distant galaxies tells us that the universe is continuing to expand, and the "big bang theory" is that favored by most scientists, although there are always new findings that may call any scientific theory into question.

When one considers just a few of the facts taught us by our scientists, however, the results are simply astounding. First, astronomical observations have shown that the galaxies are grouped in the form of clusters, and that each cluster contains an average of 100 million stars.[1] Second, even a small change in some of the physical constants present in the cosmos would have resulted in an uninhabitable universe. For example, if the early expansion rate had been less by even one part in a thousand billion, the universe would have collapsed again before temperatures had fallen below 10,000 degrees. If it had been greater by a part in a million, the universe would have expanded too rapidly for stars and planets to form. Again, if the strong nuclear force of the explosion had been slightly weaker, we would have had only hydrogen in the universe. If it had been slightly stronger, there would be only helium.[2] "The odds against a universe like ours emerging out of something like the Big Bang," writes Stephen Hawkins, "are enormous."[3] The Lord has made room for us.

Or let us move down into the mundane world that we know. On this green and blue fertile ball that we call earth, God has reserved for us and for all life a little room. Were we to ascend above the stratosphere without space equipment, we would die for lack of oxygen. Were we to dig below the earth's crust, we would burn up in the heat. Were we even to remove the thin layer of topsoil that covers our land, all life would become impossible.

1. Robert John Russell, "Cosmology, Creation, and Contingency," in *Cosmos as Creation: Theology and Science in Consonance*, ed. Ted Peters (Nashville: Abingdon Press, 1989), p. 183.

2. Ian G. Barbour, "Creation and Cosmology," in *Cosmos as Creation*, p. 130.

3. Hawkins, quoted by Barbour in "Creation and Cosmology," p. 57.

God has made room for us and provided a place for all things and creatures to flourish.

The Bible portrays God reserving room for us in terms of his conquering chaos:

> For thus says the Lord,
> who created the heavens
> (he is God!),
> who formed the earth and made it
> (he established it;
> he did not create it a chaos,
> he formed it to be inhabited!).
>
> (Isa. 45:18)

The picture we have in Genesis 1, therefore, is of God bringing order in place of chaos.

In the beginning, say the priestly writers of the chapter, the earth was *tohu wabbohu,* waste and void (v. 2). It has often been said that there is no doctrine of creation *ex nihilo* ("out of nothing") here in Genesis, and that God works with the pre-existent matter of the chaotic deep, the Hebrews simply using the language of the chaos dragon myth and unwilling to speculate on where the chaos came from. And yet, the Genesis writers are saying that there was void, nothing, and it is very difficult to picture that; how do you talk about nothing?

If we look elsewhere in the Old Testament at the use of *tohu wabbohu,* we see its immateriality. "He stretches out the north over the void," says Job, "and hangs the earth upon nothing" (26:7). *Tohu,* says Isaiah, is the nothingness and vanity of life that bears no fruit (49:4), the nothingness of those who worship false gods (41:29; 44:9). Or, in Jeremiah 4:23-26, *tohu wabbohu* is that void which is left when God takes back his creation. Therefore, if Genesis 1 is not talking about creation *ex nihilo,* it is saying something very close to it, and one gets the impression that the priestly writers are simply straining against language's limitations. In place of the void of chaos, God has created a habitable world.

The Lord, in his grace, has made room for us and for all things and creatures.

Genesis 1 further describes God's creative act in terms of the Creator limiting and holding back the great void of nothingness (cf. Ps. 104:5-9; Job 38:8-11). In verses 3-5, he gives limits to the darkness of the void and creates light. In verses 6-10, he captures the void above the solid firmament and under the disc of the earth. (All ancient Near Eastern peoples believed that the arc of the sky was solid, and that the earth was flat.) Then in verses 11-30, in place of the death inherent in the void, he creates life. And in verse 31, in place of the evil of the void, God pronounces all things good. In short, over against the evil, darkness, death, and chaos of nothingness, non-being, the void of non-creation, God creates goodness, light, life, and order, which make the being of all things possible. Despite the limitations of an ancient world-view that thought the sky was solid and the earth flat, Genesis profoundly sets forth its faith: God is the Maker of all things in heaven and on earth and under the earth. God in his grace has made our world possible. The Lord has made room for us.

And what a world it is! Our astronomers tell us that there are at least one hundred billion stars in our galaxy alone and easily a trillion such galaxies within the limits of present-day telescopes.[4] Yet even to our unaided senses are given wonders beyond counting: sunsets so glorious and constantly changing in their colors that no artist on earth could capture them; the rumblings of thunder over distant hills or the graceful trilling of a wren from a treetop; the feel of a fresh breeze against one's cheek or of wet sand under bare feet; the fragrance of a rose or of honeysuckle; the taste of a ripened peach. The senses of sight, hearing, touch, taste, and smell — God has lavished gifts to satisfy them, every gift a wonder in itself, unique and often unrepeatable.

Genesis 2 talks about the gifts God has poured out in place of the void. "And out of the ground the Lord God made to grow

4. Russell, "Cosmology, Creation, and Contingency," p. 183.

every tree that is pleasant to the sight," reads verse 9. The gift of beauty in the world is mentioned even before the gift of food!

When our now-grown son was in elementary school, he liked to collect reptiles and amphibians, and often he would come home from the dime store with one of those little turtles that were then on the market. (You cannot buy them now, because they were found to carry disease.) If you turned over one of those small turtles, you found that its breastplate was marked with intricate design, and I used to wonder when I contemplated those patterns — every one of them different — Who sees such things? Who sees the intricate patterns on the breastplate of a turtle? Other turtles? Or who sees the colors of the strange creatures that inhabit the depths of the seas? Who sees them, unless our marine scientists take pictures of them for us? Or who knows that the wings of a fly are brilliantly colored unless we look at them through a microscope? Surely the answer must be that God sees them. God loves beauty. And the result is that he has simply spilled out color and design, form and beauty over all the world. And Genesis affirms his love by saying that he created every tree pleasant to the sight.

That chapter by the writer we call the Yahwist names other gifts too: the gift of food, because the God of the Bible is always interested in our physical welfare (v. 9). It is no accident that when the Messiah comes, he tells us that God knows we need food and drink and clothing (Matt. 6:25-32), and so God provides a fertile earth and the rain for us from which those needs can be met. It is also no accident that the same Messiah feeds the hungry, and bids us give a cup of cold water in his name to the thirsty, and heals bodies and makes them whole. Contrary to those religions that urge us to escape this material world, the God of the Bible is always interested in our physical, earthly well-being.

So it is that God also gives the gift of work. "The Lord God took the man and put him in the garden of Eden to till it and keep it" (v. 15). Our work is to be both creative and preservative, says the text, the gift of a loving Lord who knows that idleness and uselessness are not paradise, that they erode the human soul, and that we must be about our Father's business of contributing to the sustenance of life on this planet if we would be fully human.

In its closing verses, Genesis 2 also names the gifts of sexual desire and companionship and marriage, that longing of the man to escape his loneliness and to share his life with one in whom he sees himself, with one who is "bone of his bone and flesh of his flesh" and therefore one with whom he can commune.

It is a travesty when verses 18-25 are interpreted to subordinate the woman to the man, and surely the feminists are right in claiming their equality with all males, for the text reads, "It is not good that the man should be alone; I will make a helper corresponding to him" (*kenegdo*, reads the Hebrew; my translation). That is one of the most merciful statements in the Bible. For it tells us that we were not created to be lonely, self-enclosed egos, fulfilling ourselves; rather, God created us to know companionship and the one flesh of joyful union. And our bodies, our sexual desire, and the subsequent marriage and family are loving gifts of a merciful God who has created the world "very good." As the Psalmist has sung,

> your children will be like olive shoots
> around your table.
> Lo, thus shall the man be blessed
> who fears the Lord.
>
> (128:3-4)

Let it also be said, however, that while Genesis 2 and Psalm 128 celebrate the good gift of marriage, Genesis 2:18 can also serve as a paradigm of the single life. Married or single, we are never whole just in ourselves; rather, we are whole in love and service and sacrifice toward others.

Other writers of the Old Testament also stand in awe of other gifts God has created in the world — for example, the gift of order. Long before the insights of modern ecology, the poet of Psalm 104:10-23 celebrated the interconnectedness of all things and life and burst out in praise, "O Lord, how manifold are your works! in wisdom you have made them all;/the earth is full of your creatures" (v. 24, NRSV). In similar fashion, a Wisdom writer could confess,

> Three things are too wonderful for me;
> four I do not understand:
> the way of an eagle in the sky,
> the way of a serpent on a rock,
> the way of a ship on the high seas,
> and the way of a man with a maiden.
> (Prov. 30:18-19)

One poet celebrated the coming of springtime:

> Lo, the winter is past,
> the rain is over and gone.
> The flowers appear on the earth,
> the time of singing has come,
> and the voice of the turtledove
> is heard in our land.
> (Song of Sol. 2:11-12)

Jeremiah knew the unfailing migration of swallow and turtledove, of stork and crane (8:7), and he saw in the fixed order of day and night the pledge of God's faithfulness (33:19-21).

When we consider the order that surrounds us in the natural world, our praise is no less forthcoming. How is it that all life is linked together in a food chain of intricate design, so ordered that the tiniest amoeba and the largest whale are given sustenance? How does that sky-blackening flock of birds manage suddenly to wheel at some invisible signal and go off in the opposite direction, without wing touching wing or foot scraping head? How do a million monarch butterflies know where to migrate every year, their colors enveloping the trees of Mexico like gold spilled from the palette of a painter? And why does a newborn child know immediately that sucking means nourishment? "O Lord, how manifold are your works! In wisdom you have made them all."

Genesis 1 names other gifts. For example, it talks about the fecundity of this life that the earth has been given, with "plants yielding seed according to their own kinds, and trees bearing fruit in which is their seed" (v. 12), with "swarms of living creatures" filling the world (v. 20), and all things dependent on God's Word and blessing: "Be fruitful and multiply," their Creator says (v. 22), without whose Word there is only void.

Charles Kingsley once wrote to a friend whom he was planning to visit. "Don't be anxious to entertain me," he said. "Put me down under any hedgerow and in two square yards of mother earth I can find mystery enough to keep me occupied for all the time I stay with you."[5] But Pulitzer Prize winner Annie Dillard has taught us that we do not need two square yards; much less will do:

> In the top inch of forest soil, biologists found an average of 1,356 living creatures . . . including 865 mites, 265 springtails, 22 millipedes, 29 adult beetles and various numbers of 12 other forms. . . . Had an estimate also been made of the microscopic population, it might have ranged up to two billion bacteria and many millions of fungi, protozoa and algae — in a mere *teaspoonful* of soil.[6]

The fecundity of the earth that the God of all life has made is almost beyond imagining.

Then to it all the Lord God has added his marvelous touches of humor. The otters in the lake at our summer home burrow through Styrofoam floats supporting boat docks, just for the fun of it. And on television they have been shown repeatedly sliding down muddy banks into water in their own version of playground slippery slides. Another example: a college roommate of our daughter owned a cat that draped itself on its stomach across a banister and then spent hours batting at its own dangling tail. Or

5. Kingsley, quoted in *The Westminster Pulpit,* vol. 5: *The Preaching of G. Campbell Morgan* (Grand Rapids: Baker Book House, 1954), p. 332.

6. Dillard, *Pilgrim at Tinker Creek* (New York: Bantam Books, 1975), p. 96.

consider the hippopotamus, says Job (40:15), or for that matter the enormous, gentle bulldog with a face like a mashed football that used to snort and snuffle at my husband's heels as he walked to work. Surely he who sits in the heavens at least chuckles to himself when he makes such creatures.

Creation Not Necessary

The most wondrous fact about it all, however, is that none of it had to be. God did not have to make the world or the universe. He does not need anything, says Acts 17:25, and he did not need to create the universe. In the play *Green Pastures*, God is portrayed as saying, "I'm lonely; I'll make me a world,"[7] but that ignores the fact that God is self-sufficient within the fellowship of Father, Son, and Holy Spirit in the Trinity. He did not need to seek some response to his love outside of his love within the Trinity. Modern panentheism has placed an emphasis on the imperative of love to seek response, and Jürgen Moltmann has written,

> Is not this the reason why the divine love pressed even beyond the Trinity? Does it not seek its "image," which is to say its response and therefore its bliss, in men and women?[8]

But as Eliphaz asks in the book of Job, "Is it any pleasure to the Almighty if you are righteous,/or is it gain to him if you make your ways blameless?" (22:3; cf. 35:5-8). The world, even a righteous world, would add nothing to God.

In similar panentheistic fashion, Sallie McFague has written that God has incarnated herself (her term) in the world, and that the world is therefore God's necessary self-expression, her "sacra-

7. *Green Pastures*, cited in James Weldon Johnson, *God's Trombones: Seven Negro Sermons in Verse* (1927; reprint New York: Viking Press, 1963), p. 17.

8. Moltmann, quoted by John Polkinghorne in *Science and Creation: The Search for Understanding* (Boston: Shambhala, 1989), p. 53.

ment" of outward and visible expression of herself.[9] Carter Heyward, on the other hand, maintains that God is incarnated in just relations and in our love and passionate longings for one another. Apart from us, there is no God. "Love is God. To god is love," she claims, and in mutual eros and passion we form the divine being.[10] Obviously, in such a view, God cannot exist without us.

So it is too in process theology, which is based on Whiteheadian philosophy and one of whose principal champions has been John Cobb. Process theology identifies God or the Holy Spirit with the process of becoming in the universe, with the goad toward novelty, which stimulates all creatures to realize new possibilities after the old ones are no longer sufficient to give zest to the enjoyment of being actual.[11] The aim of the divine goad is to promote every creature's own enjoyment through the whole process of creative evolution.[12] Thus, in this view, as God completes the world, so the world completes God, and God's primordial nature "is little more than a portfolio of potentialities."[13] The completion of God's nature requires the creation of the universe, without which God is not sufficient in himself.[14] In some forms of process theology — as, for example, in the thought of Peter Hodgson[15] — God is even more specifically defined as the shaping lure in history toward freedom for both nature and humans. But certainly, in all forms of process theology, God needs the world.

9. McFague, *Models of God: Theology for an Ecological, Nuclear Age* (Philadelphia: Fortress Press, 1987), p. 61.

10. Heyward, *The Redemption of God: A Theology of Mutual Relations* (New York: University Press of America, 1982), p. 48.

11. John B. Cobb, Jr., and David Ray Griffin, *Process Theology: An Introductory Exposition* (Philadelphia: Westminster Press, 1976), p. 59.

12. Ibid., p. 56.

13. George S. Hendry, *Theology of Nature* (Philadelphia: Westminster Press, 1980), p. 121.

14. Polkinghorne, *Science and Creation*, p. 61.

15. Hodgson, *God in History: Shapes of Freedom* (Nashville: Abingdon Press, 1989).

The Transcendence of God

The biblical writers, however, are quite convinced that God does not need the world and that while it will pass away, God will remain:

> Lift up your eyes to the heavens,
> and look at the earth beneath;
> for the heavens will vanish like smoke,
> the earth will wear out like a garment,
> and they who dwell in it will die like gnats;
> but my salvation will be for ever,
> and my deliverance will never be ended.
> (Isa. 51:6)

> Heaven and earth will pass away, but my words will not pass away. (Mark 13:31 and parallels; cf. Isa. 40:8)

It cannot be emphasized too strongly over against the many immanental theologies and philosophies of our day which make God dependent on his world that the God of the Judeo-Christian faith is transcendent and other from everything that he has made. To be sure, throughout the Bible, God works by his Word and Spirit in both nature and history. And the Old Testament is quite convinced that he took up residence in the midst of his people in the temple on Zion (Lev. 26:11) in fulfillment of his promise (Exod. 25:8; Gen. 17:7), just as the New Testament is sure that he dwells with his church in the Spirit (2 Cor. 1:22; 5:1-5). But when Solomon prays his prayer at the dedication of the temple, he says, "Will God indeed dwell on the earth? Behold, heaven and the highest heaven cannot contain thee; how much less this house which I have built" (1 Kings 8:27). There is no identification that can be made between God and the things of earth — how utterly unique, then, is the incarnation! — just as in the New Testament "the God who made the world and everything in it, he who is Lord of heaven and earth, does not live in shrines made by human hands . . . nor is he served by human hands, as though he needed anything, since he himself gives to all mortals life and breath and all things" (Acts 17:24-25, NRSV).

This is what it means to say God is "holy" — that he is other from all things, creatures, persons, and processes. "To whom then will you liken God," asks Second Isaiah, "or what likeness compare with him?" (40:18). And to show that God is totally different from his creation, the prophet proclaims that all the waters of the earth could be measured in the hollow of God's hand, and all the heavens could be spanned between his thumb and little finger (40:12). The nations of the world would be like a drop from a bucket to him and could be accounted as simply dust on a balance scale (40:15). So too, in Job, God's limitless holiness is set forth:

> Can you find out the deep things of God?
> Can you find out the limit of the Almighty?
> It is higher than heaven — what can you do?
> Deeper than Sheol — what can you know?
>
> (11:7-8)

Therefore Moses, in Deuteronomy, cautions the Israelites against finding God in anything "that is in heaven above, or that is on the earth beneath, or that is in the water under the earth" (Deut. 5:8; Exod. 20:4):

> Since you saw no form on the day that the Lord spoke to you at Horeb out of the midst of the fire, beware lest you act corruptly by making a graven image for yourselves, in the form of any figure, the likeness of male or female, the likeness of any beast that is on the earth, the likeness of any winged bird that flies in the air, the likeness of anything that creeps on the ground, the likeness of any fish that is in the water under the earth. And beware lest you lift up your eyes to heaven, and when you see the sun and the moon and the stars, all the host of heaven, you be drawn away and worship them and serve them, things which the Lord your God has allotted to all the peoples under the whole heaven. (Deut. 4:15-19; cf. vv. 23, 25)

Similarly, 1 Kings 19:11-12 is emphatic about the fact that God comes to the prophet Elijah not in the wind or earthquake or fire but in the "still small voice" of revelation. God is transcendent over his creation.

God is also qualitatively different from human beings. "I am God and not mortal," he tells Hosea, "the Holy One in your midst" (11:9, NRSV), just as Isaiah says, "The Egyptians are human and not God; their horses are flesh, and not spirit" (31:3, NRSV). Thus, God's thoughts are not our thoughts, neither are his ways our ways, for as the heavens are higher than the earth, so are his ways higher than our ways, and his thoughts than our thoughts (Isa. 55:8-9). The Psalmist therefore urges us, "Do not put your trust in princes,/in mortals, in whom there is no help" (146:3, NRSV), and Job can mourn, "For he is not a man, as I am, that I might answer him,/that we should come to trial together" (9:32).

The fact that God is totally other than human beings is, moreover, one of the bases of trust in the Old Testament:

> In God I trust; I am not afraid;
> what can flesh do to me?
>
> (Ps. 56:4, NRSV)

> "Be strong and of good courage. Do not be afraid or dismayed before the king of Assyria and all the horde that is with him; for there is one greater with us than with him. With him is an arm of flesh; but with us is the Lord our God, to help us and to fight our battles." (2 Chron. 32:7-8)

> With the Lord on my side I do not fear.
> What can mortals do to me?
>
> (Ps. 118:6, NRSV)

If one confesses the faith of the Bible, with its revelation of the living God, there is no way one can ignore the transcendence of God over his universe or identify any portion of it with him. To whom then will you compare God? asks Second Isaiah (40:25), and the Bible's answer throughout its pages is no one, no creature, no thing.

It is fully consistent with this view, therefore, that Jesus Christ, who has come from the Father and returns to the Father (John 16:28; Luke 24:51; Acts 7:55; et al.), who does the work of the Father (John 5:19) by conquering the evil, darkness, and death of the chaos (John 1:5; Mark 4:35-41 and parallels; Luke 11:20), and whose kingship is not of this world (John 18:36), is not, in his divinity, subject to the limitations of nature. His miracles, his transfiguration, his resurrection appearances, his ascension — all testify to the fact that we are dealing with more than this world and nature when we deal with him.

Implications for the Church

It is this otherness of the holy God, his absolute uniqueness over against everything that he has made, which renders all New Age and liberal monism invalid, just as it renders all attempts to understand God as a male or a female figure invalid. The Bible itself vigorously guards against understanding God as a male. If we attempt to make him a female by altering the biblical language about him, then the images of carrying in the womb, of giving birth, and of suckling almost automatically come into play. One can find such a portrayal of God, as one who has birthed the world, in a liturgy for Human Rights Week of December 1990, put out by the National Council of Churches:

> Leader: The Hovering God, who birthed the worlds and even now cradles creation in a love song, invites us from our labors into worship.
>
> People: The Holy One calls us to bear witness to her fierce love and to proclaim the promised day of favor.[16]

16. Quoted from the cover of *Monday Morning: A Magazine for Presbyterian Leaders*, 19 November 1990.

Similarly, Naomi Janowitz and Maggie Wenig produced this Sabbath prayer for Jewish women:

> Blessed is She who in the beginning, gave birth. . . .
> Blessed is She whose womb covers the earth.
> Blessed is She whose womb protects all creatures. . . .[17]

Virginia Mollenkott employs the same ideology in a discussion of the image of God as a mother eagle, which she finds in Genesis 1:2:

> The similar use of *rachapth* in Genesis and Deuteronomy makes it . . . probable that the very first image in the Bible is of God as a mother eagle fluttering over the waters as she gives birth to the universe.[18]

And Rosemary Ruether speaks of "the root human image of the divine as the Primal Matrix, the great womb within which all things, gods and humans, sky and earth, human and nonhuman beings, are generated."[19]

If God "birthed the worlds," however, the worlds are one substance with the divine, and there is no distinction between the holy God and the universe. But the biblical revelation insists that there is qualitative distinction, and the God of the Bible is transcendent over everything he has made. "Hear, O Israel: The Lord our God, the Lord is one" says Jesus of Nazareth (Mark 12:29), quoting Israel's central confession (Deut. 6:4), and that distinguishes the God and Father of our Lord Jesus Christ from all the diffuse numina that many modern religionists think to find permeating the world of nature.

God is other from his universe. He does not need it, and it is

17. Janowitz and Wenig, "Sabbath Prayers for Women," in *Womanspirit Rising: A Feminist Reader in Religion,* ed. Carol P. Christ and Judith Plaskow (San Francisco: Harper & Row, 1979), p. 170.

18. Mollenkott, *The Divine Feminine: The Biblical Imagery of God as Female* (New York: Crossroad, 1983), p. 89.

19. Ruether, *Sexism and God-Talk: Toward a Feminist Theology* (Boston: Beacon Press, 1983), p. 48.

not necessary to him. And that brings us to the question, of course, of why he made it in the first place. Paul Scherer once wrote,

> There are times when we stare with unblinking eyes at this creation of his, which every once in a while turns sour, and can't see why on earth he ever did it. And the only hint the Bible gives is that the yearning in his heart just came out that way, in the light, and the darkness, and the stars, and the green valleys, and — man.[20]

There are places in the Old Testament where the writer tries to guess at the reason for the clouds and rain:

> He loads the thick cloud with moisture;
> the clouds scatter his lightning. . . .
> Whether for correction, or for his land, or for love,
> he causes it to happen.
>
> (Job 37:11-13)

But most of the time, the biblical writers just gape open-mouthed in wonder:

> O Lord, our Lord,
> how majestic is thy name in all the earth!
>
> (Ps. 8:1, 9)

> Yonder is the sea, great and wide,
> which teems with things innumerable.
>
> (Ps. 104:25)

> Consider the lilies of the field, how they grow; they neither toil nor spin; yet I tell you, even Solomon in all his glory was not arrayed like one of these. (Matt. 6:28-29)

Why did God make such wonders?

We certainly cannot say that he made the universe just for humans' sake. Job 38:25-27 recognizes that fact:

20. Scherer, *The Word God Sent* (New York: Harper & Row, 1965), p. 135.

Who has cleft a channel for the torrents of rain,
and a way for the thunderbolt,
to bring rain on a land where no man is,
on the desert in which there is no man;
to satisfy the waste and desolate land,
and to make the ground put forth grass?

The rain and grass are given, even though no human being is present. Further, Genesis 1:31 says that God created the world "very good," but we should also note that such goodness is in God's eyes and not in ours, because there are a lot of things we would not have made — seventeen-year cicadas, for example.

What human purpose do cicadas — those locust-like creatures — fill by showing up every seventeen years? In the South, writes Annie Dillard, they appear every thirteen years. But for all that time, they "scrabble around underground in the root systems of trees in the dark and damp. . . . Then in the dark of an April night the nymphs emerge, all at once, as many as eighty-four of them digging into the air from every square foot of ground. They inch up trees and bushes, shed their skins, and begin that hollow, shrill grind that lasts all summer." The adults lay their eggs "in slits along twig bark; the hatched nymphs drop to the ground and burrow," and then they vanish from the face of the earth once again and bide their time, for thirteen more years.[21] God certainly did not create cicadas to serve our human purposes!

The Bible recognizes that is God's way with many of earth's creatures. For example, Proverbs comments on four kinds of creatures that God has made:

Four things on earth are small,
but they are exceedingly wise:
the ants are a people not strong,
yet they provide their food in the summer;
the badgers are a people not mighty,

21. Dillard, *Pilgrim at Tinker Creek*, p. 98.

> yet they make their homes in the rocks;
> the locusts have no king,
> yet all of them march in rank;
> the lizard you can take in your hands,
> yet it is in kings' palaces.
>
> (30:24-28)

Amazing creatures! Yet, if it had been up to us, we probably would have skipped the creation of at least the ants and locusts and lizards. But God saw everything that he had made and pronounced it "very good."

I wonder if it is not awe before this sheer gift of teeming life in the world that alone can prompt ecological care and cause us to value the worth of every creature and thing that God has made. In Genesis 9:3, God gives us the gift of every moving thing that lives, as well as the green plants, for our food. But that is a gift of food only, not of wanton freedom to destroy God's creations.

I also wonder if it is not awe before God's gift of life that we have lost in our present abortion crisis, or in our debates over euthanasia and assisted suicide. Karl Barth wrote concerning abortion in volume III.4 of his *Church Dogmatics,* and his words are very pertinent to our abortion of one and one-half million children in the United States every year. It is when we think that we *must* live, says Barth — not that we *may* live, as a gift of God, but that we *must* live with *our* life-style, *our* standards, *our* plans for the future — that we become willing to do anything to shield ourselves from the difficulties of a hostile life. Then we become like wolf-people, says Barth, the sovereign lawgivers, the judges, and the executioners. Then we decide that an unborn life is not human, or that we are the exceptional case, or that some unborn child has no purpose in the providence of God or cannot live a useful existence.[22] All awe before God's gift of life is lost, as it is also lost when we decide that an old person is no longer useful or worthy of medical attention or of our care and

22. Barth, *Church Dogmatics,* 4 vols., ed. Thomas F. Torrance, trans. Geoffrey W. Bromiley (Edinburgh: T. & T. Clark, 1936-69), III/4:413-23.

visitation. Pushed to its ultimate extreme, such an attitude led to Hitler's gas ovens, as Leo Alexander, the psychiatrist who represented the U.S. medical profession at the Nuremberg trials, explained: "It all began," he said, "when it was believed that there was such a thing as a life not worthy to be lived."[23] Those who know that God did not have to create our lives and universe stand awestruck and reverent before their existence, however, and cannot help but wonder why the Lord God troubled himself to make them all.

The Bible gives only one answer to the question of why God created the universe: It was not only created *through* Jesus Christ, says Colossians (1:16) and John (1:3) and Hebrews (1:2), but it was also created *for* Jesus Christ, according to Colossians and Hebrews and Ephesians (1:10). The love that the Father knows for the Son was the fount of God's creation, and he poured it forth into a world of light and order, goodness and beauty that he could pronounce "very good." And all of it was meant to serve his Son, says the Scripture, that Jesus Christ might be "pre-eminent" (Col. 1:18), and that through him God might become to all creatures their all in all (Eph. 1:23).

In short, God created the universe and all that is in it out of his love for Jesus Christ. And the purpose of the universe, then, is to declare his praise. "Let everything that breathes praise the Lord," reads the final verse in the Psalter (150:6), and the last five of the psalms in that book summon all things to such praise — elements, mountains and hills, fruit trees and cedars, beasts and cattle, creeping things and flying birds, and every condition of human being. (See Ps. 148:7-12 and the sermon on that psalm which follows.)

Perhaps Karl Barth, in the eighty-second year of his life, furnished us an example of that praise. Writing at the end of May 1968, he put this in a letter to his friends:

23. Alexander, quoted by C. Everett Koop in an address before Presbyterians United for Biblical Concerns, 196th General Assembly of the Presbyterian Church (USA), Phoenix, Arizona, 1 June 1984.

> The eighty-second year that is now behind me was a troubled one both outwardly and inwardly. But even with all the vexation, anxiety, weariness, humiliation, and melancholy, all in all I look back on it gladly and at peace.

Both he and his wife were seriously ill, he writes, and world events and directions in theology were troubling. Yet, he pens, "I can shower in cold water every morning both summer and winter. . . . I have still had my pipe (even in the hospital). And late in the evening I can take a small glass of white or red wine, or occasionally a little beer. . . . I have my dear study. . . . And we also have our small but pretty and quiet garden." He mentions his housekeeper, his physician, his children and grandchildren, his friends, a new book that has just been published. And then he ends with this:

> In retrospect I have no serious complaint about anyone or anything apart from my own failure today, yesterday, the day before, and the day before that — I mean my failure to be truly grateful. Perhaps I have some difficult days ahead, and sooner or later I certainly have the day of my death. What remains for me is that in relation to yesterday and all the days that preceded it, and all those that may follow it, and finally the last day that will surely come, I should constantly hold up before me and impress upon myself: "Forget not all his benefits."[24]

"Let everything that breathes praise the Lord," because for this, all things were created.

24. Barth, *Letters, 1961-1968,* ed. Jürgen Fangmeier and Hinrich Stoevesandt, trans. and ed. Geoffrey W. Bromiley (Grand Rapids: William B. Eerdmans, 1981), pp. 295-96.

Sample Sermon

I preached this sermon some years ago at Davidson College in North Carolina, but it is so pertinent to our subject matter that it seemed appropriate to include it here.

God the Music Lover

Scripture Lessons:

Psalm 148

Colossians 1:9-20

Let me ask you a very weighty question. Why did God make the world? Karl Barth, the great Swiss theologian, once wrote, "The miracle is not that there is a God. The miracle is that there is a world." And that is true. For if you really stop to think about it, there is no reason whatsoever for the fact that God should have made this world. James Weldon Johnson imagined in his poem about the creation that God stepped out in space and said, "I'm lonely — I'll make me a world."[1] But that conception, for all its beauty, not only ignores the

1. Johnson, *God's Trombones* (1927; reprint New York: Viking Press, 1963), p. 17.

This sermon was first published in my 1984 book entitled *Preaching as Theology and Art* (Nashville: Abingdon Press). That book is now out of print, and I hold the copyright.

fellowship of the Trinity. It also embodies our perennial conceit: we seem to feel that somehow God needed us petty human beings.

The truth is, of course, that he probably would have been a lot better off without us. We have given him nothing but trouble since he made us, and it shows the limitless patience of the Creator that he continues to bother with this world at all. Any lesser God would have washed his hands of the whole affair long ago.

And so the question remains, Why did God make the world? It is a question that philosophers and theologians have wrestled with for centuries: Why is there something? Why not nothing? Or, as Annie Dillard put it in her prize-winning book, "The question from agnosticism is, Who turned on the lights? The question from faith is, Whatever for?"[2] Why did God make this world?

Now if I may engage in just a bit of whimsy this morning, I would like to suggest that God made this world and all that is in it first of all because he is a lover, but second because he is a music lover.

When we look about us at this universe in which we live, it is not difficult to believe that God made the world because he loves. We are surrounded on every side by works of extravagant beauty and variety and intricacy. The lowly housefly bears on his wings colors of breathtaking beauty, as anyone knows who has ever looked at them through a microscope. The turtle drags along in the mud a belly plate marked with intricate pattern. The head of an ordinary caterpillar contains 228 separate and distinct muscles. And that's just speaking of very common creatures. What are we to say of wildflowers and scarlet tanagers and dogwood trees, of pink coral reefs and wooded hills and waterfalls, except that they are stamped with the love of a God wildly enthusiastic about his work? The author of Psalm 29 could even look at a thunderstorm, crashing out of the north to set woods afire and floods running and to strip trees of their leaves, and yet proclaim "Glory!" for the storm too speaks of the glory of a God exuberant about his creation. God loves his

2. Dillard, *Pilgrim at Tinker Creek* (New York: Bantam Books, 1975), pp. 147-48.

work. I like Annie Dillard's phrase: "The Creator loves pizzazz!"[3] God loves his work. And so the author of Genesis 1 could say he pronounced it "very good." And, Colossians could add, he made it through and for Jesus Christ. The love we have known in the Son of God is laid upon the world and fashions out of the stuff of nothing the marvel of creation. God made the world through his Son, the Word, because he is a lover.

But he also made the world because he is a music lover. The answer to the love of God is to be the creation's echoing praise. The whole universe is to praise its Creator for the existence he has given it, for the good life he has made. In the psalm that we heard for our Old Testament lesson, there is a universal call to praise:

> Praise him, sun and moon,
> Praise him, all stars of light . . .
> fire and hail, snow and vapor,
> stormy wind doing his word.
> The mountains and all hills,
> trees of fruit and all cedars,
> wild beasts and all cattle,
> creeping things and winged fowl. . . .
> Praise the name of the Lord,
> for he commanded and they were created.
> (Ps. 148:3, 8-10, 5, my translation)

So reads the ancient Hebrew. The response of the creation to its Creator is to be a thankful praise, a ringing hallelujah for the good life that God through his Son has made.

And God waits for that song of his creation to rise up to him, waits to hear the thankful affirmation "Yes, life is very good," waits to hear the praise and know that all is right with his world. God is a music lover who wants to hear his creation sing, because when it sings he knows that his creation is as it should be, stamped with his love and overflowing with good, in a perfection of harmony.

3. Ibid., p. 140.

All creation does try to sing a song of praise to its Maker. We think it is just poetic license and exaggeration when our psalm talks about the universe singing and praising God, or when Job speaks of the morning stars singing together. But we do now know that there is a regular energy pulsing from quasars ten billion light-years away, in a remarkable rhythm, that there is indeed a kind of music of the spheres.

I shall never forget a talk Lesslie Newbigin gave one time about the nights he spent in the jungles of India. He said the dark was full of sounds — the roar of lions and shrieks of jackals and jabbering of monkeys. "And," asked Newbigin, "who hears all these things — there in the depths of the jungle of India, night after night?" Well, God hears them. His creatures sing him songs in the night, and God loves the music and is very pleased that his creation is very good.

Ach, that's a bunch of nonsense, say our literalistic and pedantic minds. Maybe it is. But did you know that nature seems to abhor a silence, and that somewhere, underlying all the other signals, is a continual music? Lewis Thomas, the biologist, tells us, for example, that even lowly termites "make percussive sounds to each other by beating their heads against the floor in the dark, resonating corridors of their nests"; and analysis of the sound "has recently revealed a high degree of organization in the drumming; the beats occur in regular, rhythmic phrases, differing in duration, like notes for a tympani section." Bats, as we all know, make sounds almost ceaselessly to sense, by sonar, all the objects in their surroundings. But they have also been heard to produce strange, solitary, and lovely bell-like notes while hanging at rest upside down in the depths of the woods. Fish, says Thomas, "make sounds by clicking their teeth, blowing air, and drumming with special muscles against tuned inflated air bladders."[4] Animals with loose skeletons rattle them. Even leeches tap rhythmically on leaves.

We know that humpback whales sing, because recordings have

4. Thomas, "The Music of the Spheres," in *The Lives of a Cell: Notes of a Biology Watcher* (New York: Viking Press, 1974), pp. 20-24.

been made of their songs, and we rational humans have concluded that their long, complex, insistent melodies are simply practical statements about navigation, or sources of food, or limits of territory. But how strange it seems, notes Thomas, that they should send "through several hundred miles of undersea such ordinary information as 'whale here.'" Sometimes, "in the intervals between songs," they have been seen to breach and to leap clear of the waves, "landing on their backs, awash in the turbulence of their beating flippers."[5] It is as if they were showing pleasure and jubilation for the way their songs went, and yes, perhaps their praise for the joy of life.

Bird songs, of course, have been analyzed into nothing more than warning calls and mating messages and pronouncements of territory. But as Thomas has put it,

> The thrush in my backyard sings down his nose in meditative, liquid runs of melody, over and over again, and I have the strongest impression that he does this for . . . pleasure. Some of the time he seems to be practicing, like a virtuoso in his apartment. He starts a run, reaches a midpoint in the second bar where there should be a set of complex harmonics, stops, and goes back to begin over, dissatisfied. Sometimes he changes his notation so conspicuously that he seems to be improvising sets of variations. It is a meditative . . . kind of music, and I cannot believe that he is simply saying, "thrush here."[6]

Yes, all creation praises its Maker. We hear only a few of the sounds at one time, but Thomas has further suggested that if we could hear the combined sound which rises from the universe, it would lift us off our feet. But God hears it, and he is pleased. God is a music lover.

We human beings are supposed to join in the praise, of course. In the psalm that we heard for our Old Testament lesson, not only nature is called to join the song, but also

5. Ibid., p. 24.
6. Ibid., p. 22.

kings of the earth and all peoples,
princes and all rulers of the earth,
youths and also maidens,
old men and children.
(Ps. 148:11, my translation)

Indeed, the Old Testament conception is that praise is synonymous with life. In Hebrew thought, one of the chief characteristics of the dead was that they could not praise God, and that is one of the things that made the realm of Sheol, the place of the dead, so terrible. To live is to praise the Lord, according to the Bible, and if you do not praise, you are as good as dead.

Thus the biblical faith has always been a faith filled with the sound of song. From the song of Miriam at the time of the Exodus, through the songs of the Psalter, to the hymn at the Last Supper, to the singing of Paul and Silas in prison, and finally to the pictured hallelujah chorus in the kingdom of God in Revelation, those who trust are those who sing songs of praise to God the music lover. It is the chief end of man, says the Westminster Confession, to glorify God and enjoy him forever. Or, in our New Testament lesson, all things were created for Christ. We were made to praise his name, along with all creation, in songs of praise and thanksgiving.

The difficulty is, of course, that we have interrupted the praise. We have interrupted it with the still, sad song of humanity. Think what we have done to the song of praise our Old Testament lesson calls for from the old men and children. The song of the old man is now the mumbling stupor of the resident of a nursing home, in pain, alone and forgotten, and drugged so that he will keep quiet until he dies. The song of the child has become the whimpering cry of millions of hungry infants, in South America and India and famine-ridden parts of Africa, or conversely it has become the scornful laugh of irresponsibility on the lips of the overgratified youngster in America.

Or think what we have done to the song of praise from grizzly bear and coyote, from whale and manatee, from eagle and whooping crane — all those endangered species. We are slaughtering off the sound of their singing. Indeed, we human beings have ravished the world with our bug sprays and poisons and technology, with our bulldozers and concrete and earthmovers, and now the day seems not far distant when God the music lover will listen and hear from his good earth nothing but a deafening silence.

It is profound the way the prophets of the Old Testament picture the end of the world. Jeremiah talks about the time when there shall no longer be the sound of mirth and of singing, when no voice of feasting or merriment will interrupt the stillness caused by sin. His last apocalyptic picture of judgment is a picture of awful silence, when there is no bird left to sing on a bush and no human and no light. It is a picture that could very well portray our world after the final hydrogen bomb explodes. The earth is left a still, dark sphere, turning silently in space, with no sound but the whistling of that stormy wind, blowing once again over the void of chaos. Has our sin become the vast acoustical tile by which we are slowly but surely walling in the universe and creating for ourselves that ghostly and ghastly stillness? "This is the way the world ends: not with a bang but a whimper." Silence. Because we are destroying the song of praise.

I know of no way to restore the song except that one given in both our Scripture readings — to become lovers of God, because we see the love with which he has first loved us:

> Praise the name of the Lord, [reads our psalm,]
>   for exalted is his name alone.
> His majesty is over earth and heavens,
>   and he has raised up a horn [that is, salvation] for his people.
> Praise is for all his saints,
>   for the children of Israel, a people near to him.
>
> (Ps. 148:13-14, my translation)

You see, we have systematically failed to praise God for the life he has given us, and we have systematically and wantonly destroyed his good earth. But God will not have done with us! There is the final miracle — that he will not rest content with our sin and silence. He will not deliver us into the dominion of darkness and its stillness unto death. Instead, he has sent his own Son into our wasting and wasted lives, to walk this world with us, and he has said, "Here, here is the measure of my love for you; here is my forgiveness of your sin. You have laid waste my world and ignored my love, stamped on earth and sea and heavens. But you are more important to me than my sparrows, than the grass that clothes my meadows. You are of infinitely more worth than my lilies in the field."

Do you remember Jesus' teachings when he told those things to us? "Look at the birds of the air," he said. "Are you not of more value than they?" (Matt. 6:26). And "consider the lilies of the field, how they grow; they neither toil nor spin; yet I tell you, even Solomon in all his glory was not arrayed like one of these. But if God so clothes the grass of the field, which today is alive and tomorrow is thrown into the oven, will he not much more clothe you, O [you] of little faith?" (Matt. 6:28-30). God loves us even more than he loves his beloved creation.

That is a fantastic thought. God loves you more than all the wonders of his world. Think of the care he lavishes on the birds — clothing them in gorgeous colors, providing them trees for nests and infinite melodies in song, guiding their instincts year by year in their seasonal migrations, feeding them with bug and berry and giving them drink from the rain. And yet Jesus says, "Are you not of more value than they?" God lavishes on you more care and love in his Son Jesus Christ than he has lavished on all his creation through him. And so the profound and familiar hymn can sing it:

> Fair are the meadows,
> Fairer still the woodlands,
> Robed in the blooming garb of spring.
> Jesus is fairer, Jesus is purer,
> Who makes the woeful heart to sing.

God loves you more than he loves all creation. And so he gives his very Son for you on a cross to restore to you abundant life, that you may have joy and hope and learn once again what it is to sing. And Christ is raised from the dead, that you may truly have the power to love your neighbor, that woman and child and old man to whom we are to minister. Is there any one of us here so sunk into sinful and sullen silence that we cannot, that we will not praise God for such love?

But then, good Christian saints, is our feeble praise sufficient to laud the love of such a God? Or do we not, with our Psalmist, need to be joined in our praise by a universal chorus? When our voices are feeble in their song to God, do we not need the mighty whale's jubilation? When we sleep tonight, do we not need the night creatures' roars and shrieks of joy — the endangered tiger, the wolf, the Rocky Mountain grizzly? When we are inconstant, should there not be the steady pulsation of the distant stars, beaming their energy through an unpolluted sky? And when we are dissonant and divided in our praise, should not our disharmony be drowned out by the liquid melodies of lark and wren, or the roar of pure waterfalls?

Our Scripture lesson from Colossians proclaims that all things hold together in Christ. And perhaps this is finally the way we affirm that is really true — by so loving our God in his Son that we will not disrupt the song of one old man or child, that we will not still a single sparrow's song raised to him in praise, or pollute the waters of one fish that bubbles out its joy, or condone the setting out of a trap of poison for one coyote howling his hallelujah. Then indeed God's universe can be joined together as one, sounding forth its great, unbroken *Te Deum* in one united chorus of praise for the love that God has lavished upon us in his Son. And God the music lover can hear and smile and rejoice over his work, and affirm once again, as he did at the beginning, "Behold, it is very good."

And so, good Christians, praise the Lord.
Praise the Lord from the earth . . .
you young men and maidens together,

you old men and children.
Praise the name of the Lord,
for his name alone is exalted;
his glory is above earth and heaven.
He has raised up salvation for his people.
Praise is for all of you, his saints,
for you are the people who are near to him.
Therefore praise the Lord! Praise the Lord!
Hallelujah!
Amen.

CHAPTER 4

The Biblical Balance

On December 26, 1966, UCLA medieval historian Lynn White, Jr., gave an address before the American Academy for the Advancement of Science entitled "The Historical Roots of Our Ecological Crisis" — an address that has now become famous among environmentalists. In that address, White accused Christianity of deserving a huge burden of guilt for the ecological crisis. It was Western Christianity, maintained White, that furthered the idea that this earth was given explicitly for human benefit and rule; that wiped out the native animism which had empathized with the environment and used it carefully; that established a dualism between human beings and nature; and that insisted that it was God's will that humans exploit nature for their own ends.[1] White's views found a receptive audience and have persisted in many scientific, theological, and feminist circles ever since. But such views can be given credence only if we do not know the Scriptures.

1. This address was published in *Science* 155 (1967): 1203-7.

Human Beings as Glorious

Certainly if we put human beings in the perspective of the evolution of the universe, they are an insignificant species. Philip Hefner has pointed out that the universe most likely came into existence with the Big Bang about eighteen billion years ago; the earth's crust congealed about four billion years ago; dinosaurs flourished from 180 million to 63 million years ago; our important ancestor, *homo erectus*, flourished 600,000 to 350,000 years ago. Suppose, suggests Hefner, that we were to plot this sequence of events on a calendar, with one day equaling fourteen million years and one hour equaling a half-million years. Then our history would be as follows: on January 1, the earth's crust congealed; dinosaurs appeared on December 21; Neanderthal man arrived only at 11:50 p.m. on New Year's Eve. "Relative to the overall history of the natural cosmos," concludes Hefner, "the role of the human species is staggering in its minuteness."[2]

Yet, few modern scientists would not admit human uniqueness. "Life, even cellular life, may exist out yonder in the dark," wrote Loren Eiseley. "But high or low in nature, it will not wear the shape of man."[3] Or, as Lewis Thomas said in a commencement address at Stanford University, "Our place in the world is still unfathomable because we have so much to learn, but it is surely not absurd. We matter."[4]

Indeed, the Bible maintains that we matter uniquely — not supremely, but uniquely. In both of the creation accounts in Genesis, the creation of human beings stands apart. In Genesis 1, it is the high point of creation, the result of God's special planning (v. 26) and the emphasized result of his work alone (cf. the

2. Hefner, "The Evolution of the Created Co-Creator," in *Cosmos as Creation: Theology and Science in Consonance*, ed. Ted Peters (Nashville: Abingdon Press, 1989), p. 213.

3. Eiseley, *The Immense Journey* (New York: Random House–Vintage Books, 1946), p. 24.

4. This remark was reported in *The Stanford Observer*, June 1980, p. 2.

threefold use of the verb *bara'*, which is used only of God's creative activity, in v. 27). In Genesis 2, the creation of the man and the woman is the central focus of the account, with all centered around God's forming of them. Moreover, Genesis 2:7 and 2:22 emphasize the intimate nature of their creation by saying that God formed them in his hands, like a potter working with clay.

We must understand these verses in Genesis 2 correctly, however. We have in verse 7 a capsule summary of Hebrew anthropology. Human beings, it says — for it is intended to be the story of us all — are essentially flesh, material stuff, *'adam* from the *'adamah.* In short, our bodies are an essential part of our personhood, which is why Christianity talks about the resurrection of the body and not the immortality of the soul. We are flesh that must be animated. There we lie, according to verse 7, hunks of clay in the hands of our Creator, whereupon God breathes the breath of life into our nostrils and we become living beings (cf. Job 33:4; Ezek. 37:9). According to the Bible, however, it is that breath which sustains the life of all living things (Ps. 104:29-30; cf. Num. 27:16), so we are not unique on that score; God is not breathing some "soul" into us, according to this verse in Genesis. We share our dependence on the animating breath of God with all living creatures, and if God holds his breath or takes it back, we and they return to dead physical matter (Job 12:10; 34:14-15; Ps. 90:3; 146:4; Eccles. 12:7). Thus, as you read these words, your lungs are being sustained in their regular pumping by God's breath, which keeps you alive.

In short, we share a material, bodily existence with all living creatures, and we are not some sort of unique spiritual beings elevated above the rest of nature. The Scriptures are well aware of the fact that we have bodily needs and instincts, just like every other animal, and the Lord's Prayer prays that we be given our daily ration. We are physical creatures, as anyone knows when their knees start to hurt if they remain too long on them in prayer. Wrote Helmut Thielicke, "We are indifferent to the most beautiful of picture galleries when we are coming down with the grippe, and

. . . all sense of devotion trickles away when our feet are cold."[5] So, while Genesis 2 makes human beings the center of God's creation, it at the same time affirms our common nature with all living creatures.

On the other hand, Genesis 2 also affirms our difference from the world of the animals and our uniqueness in relation to them. In Genesis 2:18-20, when the Lord God seeks a helper for the man who will correspond to him, he brings all of the animals and birds to the man to see what the man will name them. "But for the man," reads verse 20, "there was not found a helper corresponding to him" (my translation). Human relationships are to be had not primarily with the world of nature but with our fellow human beings.

There is a difference between us and the animal world that sets us apart from it and, indeed, that gives us unique value in the eyes of our Maker (cf. Job 35:10-11). "Look at the birds of the air," Jesus taught. "Are you not of more value than they?" (Matt. 6:26). And "consider the lilies of the field. . . . Will [God] not much more clothe you . . . ?" (vv. 28-30; cf. Matt. 10:31; Luke 12:7). Thus, when Kenneth Cauthen writes that he finds "the notion that a mosquito has the same value as a human being simply incredible and without foundation in either Scripture or reason," the teachings of Jesus support Cauthen's view. "Reverence for all life, yes," writes Cauthen. "Equal reverence for all life, no."[6] But we have to ask, of course, what it is about us that sets us apart as unique.

Certainly the Old Testament celebrates the intimacy and care with which God has fashioned each one of us:

> For it was you who formed my inward parts,
> you knit me together in my mother's womb.

5. Thielicke, *How the World Began: Man in the First Chapters of the Bible*, translated and with an introduction by John W. Doberstein (Philadelphia: Muhlenberg Press, 1961), p. 65.

6. Cauthen, "Process Theology and Eco-Justice," in *For Creation's Sake: Preaching, Ecology, and Justice*, ed. Dieter T. Hessel (Philadelphia: Geneva Press, 1985), p. 40.

I praise you, for I am fearfully and wonderfully made.
Wonderful are your works;
that I know very well.
My frame was not hidden from you,
when I was being made in secret,
intricately woven in the depths of the earth.
Your eyes beheld my unformed substance.
(Ps. 139:13-16, NRSV)

Your hands fashioned and made me. . . .
Remember that you fashioned me like clay. . . .
Did you not pour me out like milk
and curdle me like cheese?
You clothed me with skin and flesh,
and knit me together with bones and sinews.
(Job 10:8-11, NRSV)

Yet, parts of Job 39–41 celebrate God's same care in the creation of horses and hawks, hippopotamus and crocodile:

Behold, Behemoth [hippopotamus],
which I made as I made you.
(Job 40:15)

So God's careful creation of us is not what makes us unique.

No, as we all know, human uniqueness lies in the fact that we alone of all God's creatures have been created in his image (Gen. 1:26-27). What the meaning of that concept is, however, has been endlessly debated and is by no means clear. Generally speaking, the *imago dei* has been interpreted in two ways. First, it has been interpreted as a characteristic created in human beings themselves. Thus, Calvin maintained that "at the beginning the image of God was manifested by light of intellect, rectitude of heart, and the soundness of every part."[7] S. R. Driver, in his 1904 commentary on

7. Calvin, *Institutes of the Christian Religion,* trans. Henry Beveridge (1949; reprint Grand Rapids: William B. Eerdmans, 1972), 1.15.4.

Genesis, said that the image consisted in man's self-conscious reason, including his intellectual faculties, his creative and originative power, his capability for moral transcendence, his ability for love of his fellows, and his ability for spiritual communion with God — all of which distinguished humans from the animals. Others, in the second place, have emphasized the relational character of the *imago dei,* the fact that humans can be addressed by God and respond to him, that they can stand before God and have something happen between them.

In the Old Testament itself the concept of the image is found only in the priestly writings having to do with the primeval history — in Genesis 1:26-27; 5:1, 3; and 9:6. It does not appear otherwise, and it is quite clear from the Hebrew terms used that, contrary to the New Testament's understanding, the image has nothing to do with moral perfection. Rather, the language points to the resemblance of human beings in their total person to God. The concept of the *imago dei* is a confession of the glorious nature of human beings.

The language about that glory is carefully limited and circumscribed, however. God says, "Let *us* make man in *our* image." Contrary to the belief of some, God is not addressing the Son and Holy Spirit here — the Trinity is unknown to the Old Testament writers. Rather, in Old Testament thought, God the King is addressing his heavenly court, which is made up of the heavenly beings — the seraphim, the angels, and all his heavenly hosts. (For pictures of the heavenly court, see 1 Kings 22:19-23; Job 1:6-12; Isa. 6:1-4; 40:1-8.) And God hides himself among the members of that heavenly group when he says, "Let us. . . ." So God makes us in the image of the *'elohim,* the heavenly beings, among whom he includes himself. We are something like God, but we are not directly like him. God's holy otherness is preserved, and we are not divine. (Cf. similar circumspect language in Ezek. 1:26-28. Note too how the being of God is never described in Exod. 24:9-10 or Isa. 6:1-4, just as the physical appearance of Jesus Christ is never described.) But we are glorious creatures who are something like God, a fact that is echoed in Psalm 8 and implied also in Genesis 11:6. We are the only creatures on earth of whom that is stated, and we can therefore be fully understood only within that divine-human relationship.

Furthermore, both male and female are created in God's image. The definition of humanity must include both sexes, and apart from our gender, we are not human beings. It is for this reason that Phyllis Trible's interpretation of Genesis 2:7 is rather perverse. She maintains that the creation of the "living being" in that verse refers only to the creation of a genderless "earth creature," and that sexual differentiation does not come into existence until the creation of the woman in Genesis 2:21.[8] But for the Hebrews, human nature was not human unless it was either male or female.

Genesis is very careful to say, however, that our sexuality is a part of the earthly, created order. In other words, sexuality does not belong to the transcendent God and is not of the heavenly realm. There is no marriage or giving in marriage in heaven among the angels or with God, our Lord tells us (Mark 12:25 and parallels), a point to note very carefully in our present society. There are those who maintain that sexual passion is revelatory of God, just as there have always been young couples who have believed that they have found something divine and beautiful in the backseat of a car. But sexuality and all its manifestations stem from our created state and no more reveal or contain God than do any other parts of his creation.

It is this glorious view of human nature made in the image of God that prevents every cheapening of the human personality. Surely that is a fact which every preacher should emphasize, for in our time there are many who try to make us less than we are. Bureaucrats repeatedly try to turn us into nothing more than statistics. For advertisers we can be only targeted consumers. The military reckons our humanity in the grisly figures of "body counts" and "acceptable losses." Medicine can view us as collections of

8. Trible, *God and the Rhetoric of Sexuality* (Philadelphia: Fortress Press, 1978), pp. 94-99.

cells, with DNA to be manipulated. We ourselves, on the other hand, often define our relatives and friends by what they do in their jobs — as engineers, housewives, salespersons, lawyers — and when they can no longer work, we relegate them to the status of "useless." Some among us who believe in astrology actually think we are just pawns of fate or of the stars. And of course some in our time think we are little more than sexual animals, with instincts to be heeded and satisfied no matter what the cost. Or, in the terrible language of prejudice, we are just "weepy females" or "happy darkies" or "lazy Indians" or "sneaky Orientals."

Howard Thurman, the famous black leader of a previous generation, was once asked during a television interview how he managed to achieve so much in the days when racism was written into our laws and lay like a plague over this country. "My mother kept telling me I was a child of God," he replied. It is that relationship, that relationship with God, in whose image we are made, which elevates our personhood above every lesser definition. And when society will not recognize our glorious nature and tries to make us numbers or things or animals, when the world defines us solely in economic terms or in those of race or gender or class, when we are seen as nothing more than psychological or sociological phenomena, and indeed, when someone would deny us the right of worshiping the one in whose image we are made, then revolutions break out in the attempt to reclaim our true nature — witness the women's movement or the collapse of communism in our time. There is something deep within our being that will not let us be satisfied with less than our Creator has made us — his glorious images scattered over the face of the earth. That is one side of the Bible's marvelous, balanced doctrine of human nature.

Human Beings as Creatures

On the other side, however, the Bible is quite clear that we are not gods and goddesses, a fact implied in Genesis 1 and clearly set forth in Genesis 2. There is that tree in the midst of the garden in which the Lord God has set the man and the woman. And the command is "Of the tree of the knowledge of good and evil you shall not eat, for in the day that you eat of it you shall die" (v. 17). In other words, there is a limit on our existence, a limit beyond which we must not step if we wish to have life abundant. We are creatures and not the Creator, and we are dependent on his love for us.

God's love for us is very spacious, however. "All things are yours," writes Paul, "and you are Christ's; and Christ is God's" (1 Cor. 3:21, 23). Through his love in Christ poured out for us in the creation of the world, we have been given all things needful — beauty, sustenance, daily work, companionship, intimate relationship with our Creator. And of all creatures, we are pictured in Genesis 2 as having been given the freedom to choose to live from God's abundance, to be the creatures we were meant to be in the Creator's scheme of life. We could choose to be images of God; we could choose our place and role in the world. God trusted us to make that choice in the spaciousness of our God-given freedom. But of course we would choose wisely only if we trusted God, only if we believed that he had our welfare at heart. A child will obey a parent only when the child loves the parent and trusts the parent's command. And we would obey God's command to live within the abundance of the life he has given us only if we loved and trusted him. But of course that love and trust are precisely the attitudes that will be missing in the story of Genesis 3.

The phrase "the knowledge of good and evil" in Genesis 2:17 has nothing to do with intellectual inquiry, and God is not putting some limit here on our learning and technical ability. The phrase in the Hebrew signifies the divine ability to know and to do all. Therefore, despite all of our prowess and creative capacities and abilities to shape society and nature, God is commanding us to live as the creatures we are, dependent on him for our very life. He is commanding us not to try to be our own creators and to choose in trust and love to be his creatures instead. In short, he is telling us that only in relationship with him can we live and not die.

That is the other side of the marvelous balance in the Bible's view of human nature, for the limitation prevents every proud attempt to rule nature and history in the place of God. The biblical story recounts tale after tale of such pride. "Come, let us build ourselves a city, and a tower with its top in the heavens," say the nations in the story of the Tower of Babel, "and let us make a name for ourselves, lest we be scattered abroad" (Gen. 11:4) — the picture of our human attempts to secure our own fame and security. "I am, and there is no one besides me," claims proud Babylon in Isaiah 47:8; "I shall not sit as a widow/or know the loss of children." Or there is this of King Uzziah of Judah in 2 Chronicles 26:15-16: "And his fame spread far, for he was marvelously helped, till he was strong. But when he was strong he grew proud, to his destruction." Similarly, few descriptions can match that of the proud wicked which we find in Psalm 73:

> Pride is their necklace;
> violence covers them as a garment.
> Their eyes swell out with fatness,
> their hearts overflow with follies.
> They scoff and speak with malice;
> loftily they threaten oppression.
> They set their mouths against the heavens,
> and their tongue struts through the earth.
> (vv. 6-9)

All such proud persons and nations believe that God was not serious when he told Adam and Eve not to eat of the forbidden tree. They believe, as the serpent led Eve to believe, that they will not die (Gen. 3:4). "How can God know?" ask those wicked in Psalm 73. "Is there knowledge in the Most High?" (v. 11). Or "the fool says in his heart, 'There is no God'" (Ps. 14:1 = 53:1). But everywhere throughout the Scriptures the verdict is always the same on our foolish pride that leads us to try to be our own gods and goddesses:

> Because you consider yourself as wise as a god,
> therefore, behold, I will bring strangers upon you. . . .

Will you still say, "I am a god,"
in the presence of those who slay you,
though you are but a man, and no god,
in the hands of those who wound you?
(Ezek. 28:6, 9; to Tyre)[9]

How you are fallen from heaven,
O Day Star, son of Dawn!
How you are cut down to the ground,
you who laid the nations low!
You said in your heart,
"I will ascend to heaven;
above the stars of God
I will set my throne on high;
I will sit on the mount of assembly [of the gods] in the far north;
I will ascend above the heights of the clouds,
I will make myself like the Most High."
But you are brought down to Sheol,
to the depths of the Pit.
(Isa. 14:12-15; to Babylon)

The singer of Psalm 73 describes God's judgment on the proud in these terms:

Truly thou dost set them in slippery places;
thou dost make them fall to ruin.
How they are destroyed in a moment,
swept away utterly by terrors!
(vv. 18-19)

And of course there is the judgment on us all in the picture of us all, personified in Adam and Eve, when we try to make God unnecessary and to become our own deities instead, shaping our

9. Cf. Ezek. 29:3; 31:10-11; Jer. 48:29-31; 49:16; 50:29; Isa. 16:6-7; Obad. 3-4; Zeph. 2:15; Dan. 5:20; et al.

own futures and deciding on our own what is right and wrong: "You are dust, and to dust you shall return" (Gen. 3:19). God is very serious when he tells us that apart from love and trust and obedience to him, we shall surely die.

It is for this reason that I shudder when the New Age religionists and the radical feminists tell us that we are divine, just as I also shudder when I read Dorothee Sölle's interpretation of Genesis 3:

> Coming out is liberation. Let us read the story of Adam and Eve as a coming out. The first human beings come out and discover themselves; they discover the joy of learning, the pleasures of beauty and knowledge. Let us praise Eve, who brought this about. Without Eve we would still be sitting in the trees. Without her curiosity we would not know what knowledge was.[10]

For Sölle, then, God is love within human beings: "God is our capacity to love. God is the power, the spark, that animates our love. . . . We should stop looking for God," she says. "He has been with us for a long time."[11] Therefore, according to Sölle, we are strong, we can accomplish things, we are not dispensable, we can create a new social order and a new world: "We do not have to sit around all year singing, with Luther, 'Did we in our own strength confide, our striving would be losing.'"[12] Or, she says, "To live, we do not need what has repeatedly been called 'God,' a power that intervenes, rescues, judges and confirms. The most telling argument against our traditional God is not that he no longer exists or that he has drawn back within himself but that we no longer need him. We do not need him because love is all we need, nothing more."[13] Thus has human pride eaten of the tree and tried to

10. Sölle, *The Strength of the Weak: Toward a Christian Feminist Identity*, trans. Robert and Rita Kimber (Philadelphia: Westminster Press, 1984), p. 126.

11. Ibid., p. 138.

12. Ibid., p. 158.

13. Ibid., p. 137.

make the God of the Bible unnecessary. And God's judgment on that proud attempt has always been and will always be "You are dust, and to dust you shall return."

So we have in the Old Testament a profoundly balanced view of our nature as human beings, and the pulpit needs repeatedly to preach both sides of that balance. We are glorious creatures, made in the image of God, and therefore we are never to be treated as less than that, which is the guard against all tyranny and cheapening of the human personality. But we are not gods and goddesses and are never to be regarded as such, which is the guard against all human pride and its death-dealing consequences.

The Meaning of Our Dominion

We are made in the image of God, according to Genesis 1:28, in order that we may have dominion over the earth. Some interpreters have maintained that our dominion over the earth is the essence of the *imago dei* in us. But it is more correct to say that our dominion over the earth is the result of the image. We can rule over the world because we are created in God's image. In short, we derive our ability to rule from him who is the Ruler of all, and ours is a subservient sovereignty.

Perhaps Gerhard von Rad has made this most clear in his *Old Testament Theology.*[14] In the days of the Roman empire, he suggests, an emperor could not be everywhere in his realm, and so he made little statues of himself, little images, that were erected throughout the realm in order to show that it belonged to the emperor. So too God has made us, his little images, and has placed us all over the face of the earth in order to show that the earth belongs to him. Indeed, even when we travel to the moon, we are not claim-

14. von Rad, *Old Testament Theology,* vol. 1 (Edinburgh and London: Oliver & Boyd, 1962), p. 146.

ing its territory for ourselves but rather are taking God's image there and signifying that the moon too belongs to God. The fact that we are given dominion over the earth points to God's superior dominion over it, and all we do in the world, therefore, is to point to God's rule. In the words of Jesus, "Let your light shine before others, so that they may see your good works and give glory to your Father in heaven" (Matt. 5:16, NRSV).

This is the understanding of our human place in the universe that Lynn White and those others who have blamed the Christian faith for the ecological crisis have not grasped.

To be sure, there is no doubt that Christianity has made possible much of the West's technological and scientific progress. By removing the divine from the realm of nature, the biblical faith has given the natural world to human investigation as an object that can be studied and used. For example, in India one finds a belief in karma and the unending reincarnation of a person in various forms. So a Hindu may not kill a rat because the rat might contain the soul of his grandmother, and rats therefore eat up tons of India's grain supply every year — the Christian faith makes a difference in how people live. (My aunt, who was a medical missionary in India for fifty-five years, used to say that you could smell the difference between a Christian and a Hindu village.) The difficulty, of course, is that in our human pride we have decided that we are gods and goddesses and that the creation belongs to us to do with as we like. Our ecological crisis is due not to the biblical faith but to our abandonment of that faith, and that crisis continues because of our proud and sinful belief that, having corrupted the world of nature, we now, on our own, can make it whole again.

In the Bible there is never any thought that the world and all that is in it belong to human beings. We are God's images, his stewards whose task it is to preserve and care for his earth and to distribute earth's benefits, like wine stewards preserving and caring for a wine cellar and dispensing its goodness. But we do not own the earth or anything in the universe. God owns all things:

The earth is the Lord's and the fulness thereof,
the world and those who dwell therein.
(Ps. 24:1; see 1 Cor. 10:26)[15]

For every beast of the forest is mine,
the cattle on a thousand hills.
I know all the birds of the air,
and all that moves in the field is mine.
(Ps. 50:10-11)

Gilead is mine; Manasseh is mine;
Ephraim is my helmet;
Judah is my scepter.
Moab is my washbasin;
upon Edom I cast my shoe [a sign of ownership];
over Philistia I shout in triumph.
(Ps. 60:7-8 = 108:8-9)

It is I who by my great power and my outstretched arm have made the earth, with the men and animals that are on the earth, and I give it to whomever it seems right to me. (Jer. 27:5)

In his hand are the depths of the earth;
the heights of the mountains are his also.
The sea is his, for he made it;
for his hands formed the dry land.
O come, let us worship and bow down,
let us kneel before the Lord, our Maker!
For he is our God,
and we are the people of his pasture,
and the sheep of his hand.
(Ps. 95:4-7)

God's ownership of the world is therefore recognized in Israel's laws. All firstfruits of the ground (Exod. 23:19; 34:26; Deut. 26:1-2)

15. Cf. Deut. 10:14; 1 Sam. 2:8; 1 Chron. 29:10-13; Ps. 89:11; Isa. 66:1-2.

and of animals (Exod. 34:19; cf. Num. 18:12-17) and all firstborn of human beings (Exod. 13:13, 15) were offered to God in recognition of his ownership of them, the firstborn of human beings being redeemed by the payment of a redemption price or by the service of the Levites (Num. 3:44-51). Every seventh or Sabbath year, the land was to lie fallow because God, who owned the land, commanded it (Exod. 20:8-11; 23:10-11; 31:17; Lev. 25:4; 26:34-35, 43; Deut. 5:12-15). Every Jubilee or fiftieth year, God returned the land to its original owner (Lev. 25:8-28). "The land shall not be sold in perpetuity, for the land is mine; for you are strangers and sojourners with me" (v. 23). Israel did not own the land she occupied; she was a sojourner in God's territory, a "passing guest" on God's property, as Psalm 39:12 so beautifully puts it.

Israel therefore had to care for the Lord's land and its creatures properly. Not only human beings were to have rest on the Sabbath day, but their oxen and asses and all cattle also (Exod. 20:10; 23:12; Deut. 5:14). During the sabbatical year, food left in the fields and vineyards and orchards was not only for the poor but for the wild beasts as well (Exod. 23:10-11). A calf or lamb or kid could not be taken from its mother for seven days after its birth (Lev. 22:27). If a person chanced upon a mother bird sitting on its nest or with young, the person could take the eggs or the young for food but could not take the mother (Deut. 22:6-7). And there was this provision for the time of a siege in war:

> When you besiege a city for a long time, making war against it in order to take it, you shall not destroy its trees by wielding an ax against them; for you may eat of them, but you shall not cut them down. Are the trees in the field men that they should be besieged by you? (Deut. 20:19)

God owns the things of this earth, and he commands their proper treatment. We are but his sojourners and passing guests, responsible to him for the care of his world. "The Lord God took the man and put him in the garden of Eden to till it and keep it."

Implications for the Church

The view of the Old Testament, therefore, is that if we are not obedient to the Lord of heaven and earth, we lose the land and its goodness. So it is in Genesis 3 that the primal rebellion in the garden results in the expulsion of the man and woman from the paradise that God has given them (vv. 23-24), just as Israel's rebellion in the time of the monarchy leads to exile in Assyria and Babylonia. Israel cannot defy the Lord and keep her land because the land belongs not to Israel but to God alone. Thus, in the Holiness Code of Leviticus the command is this:

> You shall therefore keep all my statutes and all my ordinances, and do them; that the land where I am bringing you to dwell may not vomit you out. (20:22; cf. 18:26-28)

The land vomits out the disobedient! And in Deuteronomy the repeated thought is that only a people who love the Lord in response to his love by cleaving to him and walking in his ways will be able to dwell long in the land which the Lord their God has given them (cf. Jer. 7:5-7; 16:12-13; 22:26; 35:15).

Indeed, any attempt by Israel to possess the land, to count it as her own rather than God's, and to believe that she therefore can live on the land as she likes is sharply reprimanded in both the law and the prophets. Deuteronomy 8:11-20 reminds Israel that the land is always gift and never possession:

> Beware lest you say in your heart, "My power and the might of my hand have gotten me this wealth." You shall remember the Lord your God, for it is he who gives you power to get wealth. (8:17-18; cf. 26:15)

Both Micah (2:2) and Isaiah (5:8-10) pronounce judgment on those who covet fields and seize them, as if the land belonged to them, to make themselves wealthy. And there is this in Ezekiel:

> Son of man, the inhabitants of these waste places in the land of Israel keep saying, "Abraham was only one man, yet he got possession of the land; but we are many; the land is surely given us to possess." Therefore say to them, Thus says the Lord God: You eat flesh with the blood, and lift up your eyes to your idols, and shed blood; shall you then possess the land? You resort to the sword, you commit abominations and each of you defiles his neighbor's wife; shall you then possess the land? Say this to them, Thus says the Lord God: . . . I will make the land a desolation and a waste; and her proud might shall come to an end; and the mountains of Israel shall be so desolate that none will pass through. Then they will know that I am the Lord. (33:24-29)

Far from being the source of our ecological crisis, the biblical understanding of our dominion over the earth, as stewards of God's land and servants of his will, should act as a powerful check on all of our proud attempts to claim that we can do with the natural world as we will. No, we cannot. "The earth is the Lord's and the fulness thereof," and we are always responsible to him. Everything that surrounds us in the natural world — its beasts, its fishes, its birds, its plants — all belong to the Lord of nature who lends them to us as gifts, and our treatment of every species and subspecies must take account of the will of the One who made them.

In this connection, it is therefore very interesting to note what the Bible believes to be the source of pollution in the world. When we think of pollution, we of course talk about toxic wastes and fertilizers polluting our waterways, about carbon monoxide from automobiles polluting our air, about factory emissions spilling forth their poisons, and about insecticides spoiling food supplies. And those are indeed serious scourges inflicted on modern life. But the Bible goes to the heart of the matter, and instead of talking about types of pollution, it talks about pollution's source. Listen to Isaiah:

> The earth lies polluted
> under its inhabitants;

for they have transgressed the laws,
violated the statutes,
broken the everlasting covenant.
Therefore a curse devours the earth,
and its inhabitants suffer for their guilt;
therefore the inhabitants of the earth are scorched,
and few men are left.
The wine mourns,
the vine languishes,
all the merry-hearted sigh.

(24:5-7)

What is it that pollutes the earth, according to the prophets? It is idolatry and the failure to serve and worship God. "They have polluted my land with the carcasses of their detestable idols," God says in Jeremiah, "and have filled my inheritance with their abominations" (16:18; cf. 2:7; 3:1, 9). Disobedience pollutes the land, according to Numbers 35:33 and Ezekiel 36:18, as does the shedding of the blood of the innocent. In short, pollution takes place when the Lordship of God is ignored and when we no longer believe ourselves responsible to him. Then we become our own gods and goddesses, or we manufacture our own idols, and the world becomes the place where our will rules supreme and we can do with the creation and other human beings anything we like.

In the light of this biblical insight, it is ironic, therefore, that many writers in our day who are urging upon us ecological responsibility are also those who are urging that we turn to the worship of a Mother Goddess or the Queen of Heaven or Isis or some other pagan deity. These days our land is full of those urging us to go after other gods that we have not known, just as it is full of those telling us that the biblical commandments can be broken with impunity. But the Bible's view is that true stewardship of God's good earth has its base in obedience and trust in the one true God. And human dominion over the earth, in the biblical understanding, finally involves life-styles and actions that point to and glorify God's sovereignty over all that he has made. Contrary to the contemporary worshipers of other gods and goddesses, we cherish and keep the earth not because the earth or any part of its environment is divine, but because it is a merciful gift entrusted to us from the Lord to whom all things belong.

Such is the marvelous balance that the Scriptures bring to our understanding of ourselves as human beings. We are glorious creatures, made in the image of God, who are never to be understood apart from or denied the necessity of that relationship, and who therefore cannot be classified or treated as just one more animal species. As such glorious creatures, we are given dominion over the earth, to care for and rule it on behalf of its owner, God. But on the other side of the balance scale, we nevertheless are merely creatures. We are not gods and goddesses. And everything we do on the earth is to point to the sovereignty of the one God and to further the will of the one Lord who made heaven and earth.

Sample Meditation

I preached this brief meditation during a twenty-minute chapel service in Watts Chapel of Union Theological Seminary in Virginia. The AIDS crisis was just beginning to become alarming in this country (the statistics in the meditation represent that beginning), and this meditation was an attempt to call students and faculty to a biblical stance toward that crisis, using the biblical understanding of the limits of human freedom.

Our Best Hope?

Scripture Lessons:

Genesis 2:7-9, 15-17

Deuteronomy 5:29-33

1 Corinthians 4:1-2

All of us are familiar with the Surgeon General's report on AIDS that came out at the beginning of last November. And all of us have some familiarity with the deadly arithmetic of that modern black death which is now eating its way through the world. Fifteen thousand persons in the United States have already died from the disease, and it is estimated that over one million Americans are now infected with the virus. By 1991, it is projected that there will be 179,000 deaths from AIDS in this country alone, not to mention the thousands dying in Haiti and Africa. The disease is, said the Committee on a National Strategy for AIDS, "potentially on its way to becoming a catastrophe that could affect the whole of American society," and indeed, the world.

As a result, the Committee has recommended that we spend $1 billion annually for research and $2 billion annually for AIDS health care. And the Surgeon General has asked that from the third grade on, your children and my grandchildren be educated in the details of so-called safe sex. Said the committee, "For now, our best hope for dealing with the problem is by launching a massive, continuing campaign to increase awareness of how persons can protect themselves against infection, such as by using condoms and avoiding . . . drug injection equipment."

Our best hope, the health experts are telling us, lies with education. Well, certainly that educational campaign must take place. But is that not a statement of a desperate hope that should bring the Christian church to its knees in shame and repentance?

Where is the voice of the church as we confront this international crisis? As you well know, AIDS is being spread in this country and around the world primarily by promiscuous sexual conduct, and the church has not had too much to say on that subject lately, has it? Indeed, very often the church has given the impression that it condones such conduct. Recently the Episcopalian House of Bishops could not bring itself to agree that sexual relations should be confined to one's marriage partner. And most people seem to assume that it is unrealistic to expect college students not to fornicate. Certainly many modern clergy would hesitate to label sexually active students as sinful. On the abortion front, most denominations have supported pro-choice, which is often used as an escape route from the consequences of extramarital sexuality. Many in the church have considered it too harsh to ask homosexuals to remain celibate, as we used to ask all unmarried persons to remain. As for AIDS, the only thing the Presbyterian Church (USA) has managed to say is that it is not a judgment from God. And whether one agrees with that statement or not, one has to ask, How do they know? No, the church has not had too much to say about promiscuous sexuality.

The Scripture verses that we heard from 1 Corinthians tell us that we Christians are the stewards of the mysteries of God, required to preserve those mysteries and to hand them on faithfully to each generation. And one of those mysteries makes up the lesson that we heard from Genesis 2 this morning.

There are limits on human life, says our passage from Genesis — limits of thankful and willing obedience owed to God. We are not independent creatures, free to do anything we wish. We are not sovereign centers of self-will for whom anything goes. No, we are subjects of a sovereign Lord who has intended that we live by his commandments. That is the way human life is created. That is built into the structure of the universe.

And you see, when the Lord God created us, he wanted so much for us to understand, and so he gave us his Word. Beloved children, he said to us, I want so much for you to live an abundant life, full of all the delights of my good earth, my gift to you. And so please, please listen to me. There is a tree in the midst of the garden called disobedience. And if you eat of the fruit of that tree, the outcome of your eating will be death. For example, if you hate one another, you will destroy your family and community and world. If you care only for yourself, you will disrupt your home and fail your children. If you despoil my good earth, you will end up with nothing but ugliness and want. And yes, if you do not properly use your bodies and respect those of your spouse and neighbor, which I have created, you will surely die.

Can we be aware of the love in that statement — of the yearning of a God who wants so much for us to have life and have it more abundantly? "Oh that they had such a mind as this always," God cries out in Deuteronomy, "to fear me and to keep all my commandments, that it might go well with them and with their children for ever!" God forbids premarital, extramarital, promiscuous sexuality to us because he wants it to go well with us and with our children forever.

Is that not part of the message which we need to go out and tell to the church and the world in our troubled time? — that God loves us, that he wants us to live, and so he has given us commandments about how to use our bodies? Is that not what the church should be saying in the face of this epidemic of AIDS now threatening so many of God's beloved people?

There are limits on human life built into the structure of creation. That is one of the mysteries of God. You and I, as Christians, are stewards of that mystery, called by God to proclaim it in our world. And it is required of stewards that they be found trustworthy. Amen.

CHAPTER 5

Contingency and Providence

We live in a contingent universe. Whether we are speaking in cosmic terms of the Big Bang and the formation of the galaxies, or in microcosmic terms of quarks and electrons, we live in a contingent universe. There is no reason for things to be as they are. The infinitesimal moment before the Big Bang, when time equaled zero and there was only singularity, is inaccessible to our science, just as the resulting order of both higher and lower levels of existence can be explained only by observing it, and cannot be deduced as the inevitable outworking of what precedes it. And of course, the changes and the novelty that we experience in the history of both nature and human beings defy precise scientific prediction.[1]

We could regard such contingency from the standpoint of scientific materialism and maintain, as does Richard Dawkins, that it is all the result of chance. The universe, he thinks, represents "the spontaneous arising of order, complexity and apparent design," despite the "astronomically long odds" against such things happening.[2] In such a view, human life and that of nature would

1. Ian Barbour, *Religion in an Age of Science,* the Gifford Lectures, vol. 1 (San Francisco: Harper & Row, 1990), pp. 145-46.

2. Dawkins, cited by Barbour in ibid., p. 179.

remain essentially meaningless. Or we can read the first words of Genesis and enter into its confession of faith: "In the beginning, God. . . ."

Why is there something — why not nothing? Philosophers and metaphysicians and theologians have asked that question for years, and the answer of biblical faith has always been, "In the beginning, God. . . ." All is the result of his creative act. Everything depends on his free will. Astrophysicist Robert Jastrow put it this way in a statement that is now famous:

> At this moment it seems as though science will never be able to raise the curtain on the mystery of creation. For the scientist who has lived by his faith in the power of reason, the story ends like a bad dream. He has scaled the mountains of ignorance; he is about to conquer the highest peak; as he pulls himself over the final rock, he is greeted by a band of theologians who have been sitting there for centuries.[3]

"In the beginning, God. . . ." We walk his earth. We breathe his air. We see his stars. We live in his complex order of nature and history. And everything finally has to be understood in relation to him. It is this which the Bible confesses with its doctrine of creation *ex nihilo*, that "all things were made through him [Jesus Christ]," and that "without him was not anything made that was made" (John 1:3). Indeed, the Bible does not even have a word for nature, because apart from God's creative act, nature has no existence.

The Dependent Creation

What we must realize is that creation, in the Bible's view as well as in that of modern science, is not a one-time act. To be sure,

3. Jastrow, *God and the Astronomers* (New York: W. W. Norton, 1978), p. 116.

Genesis 2:1 states, "The heavens and the earth were finished, and all the host of them," and there is a sense in which the universe is now there as an object with which God can work. But the Bible is also quite aware of the fact that the cosmos and all its functioning remain dependent on God's continuing action.

There is no Deism in the Bible. Sibley Towner has written that God does not run the world on a day-to-day basis, but rather that the world "operates according to the ancient orders of creation which have produced the life that teems here and elsewhere."[4] In other words, God has created all the laws by which everything happens and then left them to operate mechanically; God is like some great watchmaker, winding up the universe and then letting it tick away. And that is Deism, and it has no relation to the biblical view. Calvin recognized that long ago. "It were cold and lifeless," he writes in the *Institutes,* "to represent God as a momentary Creator, who completed his work once for all, and then left it. . . . The presence of the divine power is conspicuous, not less in the perpetual condition of the world than in its first creation."[5]

The Old Testament acknowledges the continuing dependence of the universe on God by saying, first of all, that chaos — the void, non-being, nothingness — can return. Leviathan can be roused, says Job (3:8), and the world is constantly threatened by that possibility:

> The floods have lifted up, O Lord,
> the floods have lifted up their voice,
> the floods lift up their roaring.
>
> (Ps. 93:3)

Indeed, according to the priestly view of the flood in the time of Noah, the chaos did return to annihilate all life (Gen. 7:11). And

4. Towner, "The View from the Screened-In Porch," in *Best Sermons* 1, ed. James W. Cox (San Francisco: Harper & Row, 1988), p. 160.

5. Calvin, *Institutes of the Christian Religion,* trans. Henry Beveridge (1949; reprint Grand Rapids: William B. Eerdmans, 1972), 1.16.1.

Jeremiah's vision of God's final eschatological judgment is of chaos returned:

> I looked on the earth, and lo, it was waste and void [*tohu wabbohu*];
> and to the heavens, and they had no light.
> I looked on the mountains, and lo, they were quaking,
> and all the hills moved to and fro.
> I looked, and lo, there was no man,
> and all the birds of the air had fled.
>
> (4:23-25)

Thus it is only because God holds in check the chaos, symbolized by the waters of the great *tehom* (deep), that the creation continues to exist:

> Thou didst set a bound which they should not pass,
> so that they might not again cover the earth.
>
> (Ps. 104:9; cf. Job 38:8-11; Jer. 5:22)

In short, the very structure of our universe is dependent on God sustaining its existence, as Genesis 1 acknowledges at the very beginning. It is because God rules the forces of chaos and darkness, nothingness and void, that this contingent universe continues to exist:

> Mightier than the thunders of many waters,
> mightier than the waves of the sea,
> the Lord on high is mighty!
>
> (Ps. 93:4)

Therefore, we need not fear, "though the mountains shake in the heart of the sea;/though its waters roar and foam,/though the mountains tremble with its tumult" (Ps. 46:2-3), which is the same faith that our Lord bid his disciples have when he manifested the power of God by stilling the storm, the wind, and the sea (Mark 4:35-41 and parallels; see the following sermon on this text).

The Bible, however, goes beyond God's control of the chaos in speaking of his sustaining of his creation. Ezra's prayer in Nehemiah 9:6 summarizes the Bible's thought:

> Thou art the Lord, thou alone; thou hast made heaven, the heaven of heavens, with all their host, the earth and all that is on it, the seas and all that is in them; and thou preservest all of them.

According to the Bible, it is God who ordains and controls the appearance and movement of the constellations and other heavenly bodies (Job 38:31-33; 9:7); who determines how many stars there are and gives them names (Ps. 147:4; Isa. 40:26); who makes the moon and sun to mark the seasons (Gen. 1:14; Ps. 104:19) and tells the sun to rise or set (Ps. 104:19); who apportions light and darkness, day and night (Job 38:12-13; Ps. 104:20; Amos 5:8), for animals and human beings alike. As G. K. Chesterton once remarked, "The sun doesn't rise by natural law; it rises because God says, 'Get up and do it again.'"

It is no wonder, therefore, that the heavenly bodies can be instruments of God, who can seal up the stars (Job 9:7), turn aside the heat of the sun (Ps. 121:6), cause the sun and the moon to stand still (Josh. 10:12-13; Hab. 3:11), and turn the shadow of the sun back ten steps on the dial of Ahaz (Isa. 38:7-8). God can bring darkness between the pursuing Egyptians and the fleeing Israelites at the exodus (Josh. 24:7), just as he can use darkness as an instrument of his judgment (Isa. 5:30; Amos 8:9). And so, at the crucifixion of our Lord, there is darkness over the whole land, from the sixth hour to the ninth, while the sun's light fails (Luke 23:44-45). The heavenly bodies are dependent on their Creator for their existence and their movement, and so all in our day who believe in astrology and follow the zodiac, or all in Israel who worshiped the heavenly bodies, are condemned in the writings of the prophets and the law (Isa. 47:12-13; Deut. 17:2-7; 2 Kings 21:5; 23:5, 11; Jer. 7:18; 8:1-2; Ezek. 8:16; Zeph. 1:5; et al.). Indeed, Genesis 1 makes sport of the Babylonian worshipers of the heavenly bodies by adding, in verse 16, "he made the stars also," as if the stars were just a little afterthought on the part of the Lord of creation.

But this Lord of heaven and earth also controls and sustains earth's geology, according to the Bible. He can form the mountains (Amos 4:13) or remove them (Job 9:5; cf. Amos 1:2; Mic. 1:3-4). He can lift up every valley and make low the mountains and hills (Isa. 40:4). He can cause the land to heave up and then sink (Amos 8:8; 9:5). At his presence the mountains quake (Judg. 5:5; Ps. 18:7; 68:8; 114:4-6; Isa. 64:3; Hab. 3:6, 10; Nah. 1:5), and the whole earth trembles (Judg. 5:4; 2 Sam. 22:8; Ps. 68:8; Ezek. 3:12). So it is, once again, that at the moment that our Lord dies on the cross, the earth shakes, the rocks are split, and the tombs are opened (Matt. 27:51-52), just as on the day of resurrection, an earthquake occurs as the angel descends from heaven to roll back the stone at the entrance to the tomb (Matt. 28:2).

In the Bible's view, God also sustains and controls meteorology. Sometimes described as the Rider on the clouds or wind (Deut. 33:26; Ps. 18:10 = 2 Sam. 22:11), God's appearance at his theophanies is always said to be accompanied by profound meteorological disturbances (Exod. 19:16; Ps. 18 = 2 Sam. 22; Ps. 68:7-8; 77:16-18; 97:2-4; 144:5-7; Ezek. 1; Hab. 3). He controls nature's wind (Job 1:19; 38:24; Ps. 48:7; 147:18; Jer. 10:13; Amos 4:13; Jon. 1:4; 4:8) and the elements of snow, hail, dew, and hoarfrost (Judg. 6:36-40; Job 37:5-10; 38:22-23, 28-30, 34-38; Ps. 147:16-17). Above all, in the arid land of Palestine, God can give the rain (Deut. 11:14; 1 Sam. 12:17-18; Job 5:10; 36:27; 37:6; Ps. 68:9; 104:10; 147:8; Jer. 5:24) or withhold it (1 Kings 8:35; 17:1; 2 Chron. 7:13; Isa. 5:6), and so it is he who can bring the judgment of famine upon the land (Isa. 14:30; Jer. 14:1-10; et al.). Or, as punishment for lack of faith, he can ruin the wheat harvest with rain at the improper time (1 Sam. 12:17-18). In fact, in one of Amos's oracles, God uses his control of the rain and the resulting famine as a means of discipline:

"I gave you cleanness of teeth in all your cities,
    and lack of bread in all your places,
yet you did not return to me," says the Lord.
"And I also withheld the rain from you
    when there were yet three months to the harvest;
I would send rain upon one city,
    and send no rain upon another city;
one field would be rained upon,
    and the field on which it did not rain withered;
so two or three cities wandered to one city
    to drink water, and were not satisfied;
yet you did not return to me," says the Lord.
(Amos 4:6-8; cf. Hag. 2:17)

By his control of precipitation, God makes the plants and grass grow for human beings and animals (Deut. 11:15; Ps. 104:14; 147:8; Jon. 4:6), and the Old Testament writers go even further to say that all things have their food from his hand (Job 38:39-41; Ps. 104:27-28). As the Psalmist says,

The eyes of all look to thee,
    and thou givest them their food in due season.
Thou openest thy hand,
    thou satisfiest the desire of every living thing.
(145:15-16)

Psalm 104:20-21 acknowledges the order of predation and of the natural food chain, but finally that order is ordained and sustained by God alone:

Thou makest darkness, and it is night,
    when all the beasts of the forest creep forth.
The young lions roar for their prey,
    seeking their food from God.

Over against our customary views in which the universe is a closed and secular system, allowing no place for the action of God, the Bible's confession is that the functioning of all nature is dependent on God's action. He orders the change of seasons and day and night and cold and heat (Gen. 8:22; see the meditation on this text). He apportions the time of harvest (Jer. 5:24) and the regularity of nature's ways (Jer. 18:14; Ps. 104). He makes covenant with the stones of the field and the beasts, so that all is properly ordered, and the lowliest ox knows him as its owner and the ass as its master (Isa. 1:3) — thus there is an ox and an ass in every Christmas crèche.

The order that God sets into the universe is a sign of his faithfulness (Jer. 31:35-37; 33:19-22; Zeph. 3:5). And the fact that he has made the universe and sustains it in its orderly round distinguishes him from every other deity (1 Chron. 16:26; Ps. 95:3-5; 96:5; 135:5-7; 136:4-9; Isa. 37:16; Jer. 10:11-16; Acts 17:22-27), just as his work in nature and his knowledge of nature distinguish him from all human beings (Job 38:12-41; 39:1-27; 40:15-24; 41:1-10). Therefore, in the Revelation of John, the saints sing,

> "Worthy art thou, our Lord and God,
> to receive glory and honor and power,
> for thou didst create all things,
> and by thy will they existed and were created."
>
> (4:11)

Because all nature is contingent on the action of its Lord, he can therefore use natural means to bless the righteous or to curse the unrighteous, and the long lists of blessings and curses that we find in Leviticus 26 and Deuteronomy 28 are litanies confessing God's rewards and punishments wrought by means of the natural world (cf. Exod. 23:25-26; Lev. 25:18-19; Deut. 30:8-10; 33:13-16; 2 Chron. 31:9-10; Isa. 58:9-11; Hag. 1:9-11; et al.). Indeed, in the Bible's testimony, those of faith do not doubt that God will furnish them with the goods of the natural world (cf. Ps. 37:25). "Seek first his kingdom and his righteousness," Jesus teaches, "and all these things shall be yours as well" (Matt. 6:33). And Paul writes to the Corinthians, "God is able to provide you with every blessing in abundance, so that you may always have enough of everything. . . . He who supplies seed to the sower and bread for food will supply and multiply your resources" (2 Cor. 9:8, 10).

Along the same line, the Royal Psalms are quite sure that the long-awaited, righteous, Davidic king will bring not only spiritual and political blessings to his people but also those of natural abundance (Ps. 72; 132:15).

To be sure, both Old Testament and New know that there is no automatic correlation between righteousness and natural goods. Righteous Job loses everything, and faith always presses on beyond material awards, so that Habakkuk can sing his magnificent song of faith:

> Though the fig tree do not blossom,
>   nor fruit be on the vines,
> the produce of the olive fail
>   and the fields yield no food,
> the flock be cut off from the fold
>   and there be no herd in the stalls,
> yet I will rejoice in the Lord,
>   I will joy in the God of my salvation.
>
> (3:17-18)

That is the same faith which Paul confesses when he writes that he knows how to be abased and how to abound; in any and all circumstances he has learned the secret of facing plenty and hunger, abundance and want, for he can do all things in the Lord who strengthens him (Phil. 4:12-13). Above all, the life of Jesus, who had no place to lay his head (Matt. 8:20 and parallels), and his death on the cross testify to the lack of correlation between goodness and God's bestowal of nature's bounty. Yet, no one of the faithful in the Bible doubts that nature's riches come from God. "I have no good apart from thee," prays the Psalmist (16:2). All good things, including nature's ways and gifts, come from the Lord (cf. Eccles. 2:25).

Implications for the Church

In the light of nature's dependence on God, it should not surprise us that the Scriptures are full of accounts of what we call miracles — that is, of acts and events that seem to us to violate the orderly ways of the natural world as we have come to know it: all of those plagues on Egypt in the book of Exodus and the crossing of the Sea of Reeds and of the Jordan; the wondrous happenings connected with the prophets Elijah and Elisha, as well as many other marvelous events told us in the Old Testament; the healings wrought by Jesus, and his casting out of demons; his raising of the dead and his feeding of the multitudes. The Gospel writers all have passages summarizing Jesus' marvelous acts (see Mark 1:34; 3:7-12; Matt. 14:34-36; 15:29-31; Luke 4:40-41; 6:17-19; 7:21; John 20:30-31), besides telling of his specific wondrous deeds. And the disciples continued to work Jesus' miracles, according to the Acts of the Apostles, doing signs and wonders among the people (2:43; 6:8; 8:6-7; 9:34; 14:3; 15:12; 28:8):

> Now many signs and wonders were done among the people by the hands of the apostles. . . . They even carried out the sick into the streets, and laid them on beds and pallets, that as Peter came by at least his shadow might fall on some of them. The people also gathered from the towns around Jerusalem, bringing the sick and those afflicted with unclean spirits, and they were all healed. (5:12, 15-16)

Or there is this of Paul:

> God did extraordinary miracles by the hands of Paul, so that handkerchiefs or aprons were carried away from his body to the sick, and diseases left them and the evil spirits came out of them. (19:11-12)

Since God is the Lord of the natural world, he can use it as he wills to carry out his purpose. There really is no understanding in the Bible of "miracles," as we define them — that is, as the disruption of or interference in the orderly laws of nature. In fact, there is no "natural law" in our sense of the term. Nature continues in its orderly ways because those ways are faithfully upheld and sustained by God. And the real "miracles," in the biblical view, are the faithfulness of God in his working with earth, skies, and seas, and his constant care and concern for all, including human beings:

> When I look at your heavens, the work of your fingers,
> the moon and the stars that you have established;
> what are human beings that you are mindful of them,
> mortals that you care for them?
> (Ps. 8:3-4, NRSV; cf. Job 38–41)

Nevertheless, we have to ask in our twentieth century how to regard such accounts and how to deal with them in our preaching and teaching. One of the worst possible approaches we can take to the Bible, of course, is to try to naturalize it, to demythologize it, to take our scientific frame of reference and to try to squeeze all of the Bible's marvelous accounts into that constricting and absolutized frame. We once had a visiting theologian speak at Lancaster Theological Seminary who maintained that all of Jesus' healings could now be accomplished with the use of tranquilizers and other medicines.

In an article in the magazine *First Things*, Peter Berger reflected on the loss we risk if we try to turn science into metaphysics:

> Granted (as I think we must) that modern science has given us new and often penetrating insights into reality and that modern technology has enormously increased our control over our lives, is it not possible that in the process some very precious things have been lost? . . . I am thinking of truths that may have been lost in the process. Our ancestors didn't know about particle physics, but they spoke with angels. . . . Could it be that we lost a truth when our conversation with angels came to a stop? Are

> we, can we be, so sure that the truths of modern physics necessarily imply the untruth of angels? I am not sure at all; indeed, I am strongly inclined to believe the opposite.[6]

"The Gospel is not of this world," Berger concluded, "and to try to make it so is to lose it and to lose the redemptive power it contains."[7]

That is what one sees so clearly in a commentary like that of G. A. F. Knight on the book of Exodus. Knight takes all of the miraculous events surrounding Israel's deliverance from Egypt and turns them into natural happenings. When, in Exodus 4:3, Moses' staff becomes a snake, Knight comments, "It may well be that Moses had looked at his staff from an odd angle, or contemplated the horror should his staff actually be a snake. But God made use of Moses' mental illusion, if it was such, to his glory."[8] Or concerning Moses' leprous hand in 4:6, Knight explains, "It may be that he slipped and fell on the rocks, to find his arm numb and turned white. For a moment he may have imagined that he was smitten with the dread disease of leprosy."[9] The plague on Egypt's domestic animals "may have been any one of a number of diseases, such as anthrax or foot-and-mouth disease."[10] The plague of darkness was a sandstorm.[11] The slaying of the Egyptian firstborn may have been infantile diarrhea, and "our information that *only* the first-born, and not the fourth or sixth-born, consistently caught the disease, may well be attributed to pious story-telling."[12] Thus is Exodus's testimony to the sovereignty of God over nature and nations reduced to an account of mental illusion and the spread of germs.

6. Berger, "Worldly Wisdom, Christian Foolishness," *First Things*, no. 5, August/September 1990, p. 20.

7. Ibid., p. 21.

8. Knight, *Theology as Narration: A Commentary on the Book of Exodus* (Grand Rapids: William B. Eerdmans, 1976), p. 28.

9. Ibid., p. 29.

10. Ibid., p. 67.

11. Ibid., p. 80.

12. Ibid., p. 89.

It also is no solution to try to demythologize the Bible by limiting all of its transcendent witness to a new existential self-understanding, in the manner of Rudolph Bultmann. For Bultmann, the natural world is really a closed system of cause and effect, and faith really has to do only with self-understanding. An accident can be seen as God's punishment or chastisement, or simply as a link in the chain of the natural course of events. But faith has to do only with our understanding of the accident. Similarly, the resurrection of Christ was not an observable event but the rebirth of faith in Christ among the disciples.[13] But beyond our understanding of the Bible's events — and how often we strain and wrestle to understand them and do not succeed — there must be an objective given to God's actions in the world, or faith has no foundation. As Paul says, "If Christ has not been raised, your faith is futile and you are still in your sins" (1 Cor. 15:17). We must not only believe that Christ was raised from the dead; he must also in reality have been raised.

Yet the Bible's witness does not scientifically nail down that reality for us. Every biblical account of miracles has its ambiguous side. "He is possessed by Beelzebul," the scribes charged when Jesus cast out demons, and the crowds and even Jesus' family thought he was out of his mind (Mark 3:20-31 and parallels). "Prove to me that you're no fool;/walk across my swimming pool," sings Pilate in *Jesus Christ Superstar.* But Jesus preaches, "An evil and adulterous generation seeks for a sign, but no sign shall be given to it except the sign of Jonah" (Matt. 16:4 and parallel). Somehow it is only when we experience the power of God in the risen Christ to heal us and transform our lives, to guide us continually and overcome every natural and historical obstacle to our blessedness that we know — know beyond all necessity of scientific proof — that not a sparrow falls to earth without his will (Matt. 10:29), that his is the final power over all of nature's

13. Ian Barbour provides a good summary of Bultmann's approach in *Religion in an Age of Science,* pp. 154-55.

working, and that, as Thielicke has written, "He not only 'comforts' his followers who are at the point of capsizing in their little boat, but with sovereign freedom he also commands the waves and all the elements."[14]

As we saw in the first chapter, the Bible's theology of creation grows out of its theology of redemption, and so in John 9, when the Jews doubt that Jesus has healed the man born blind and hold that no sinner could do such a deed, the man replies, "Whether he is a sinner, I do not know; one thing I know, that though I was blind, now I see" (v. 25). "I once was lost, but now am found; was blind and now I see." It is that experience which turns the whole of the natural world into the sphere of God's working and glory, and so we have in the Christian faith the doctrine of God's providence, of his continual sovereignty over and working within both the natural and the historical realms.

The Limits of Our Description

I do not think, however, that it is possible to develop a metaphysics or theological system that fully explains *how* God works in the natural world. Certainly there are many profound thinkers who have tried. Some have built on Thomas Aquinas's view of primary and secondary causes, though they have altered it in many and various ways. God, as primary cause of nature's life, works through the secondary causes, which science describes. Others have framed their thought in terms of God's self-limitation over against the natural world, with God working like an artist with a medium of wood or stone that has its own nature, or with God acting like a parent of a growing child, persuading and directing but never coercing. The linguistic analysts speak in terms of the distinction between causation and intention, and encompass the natural

14. Thielicke, *I Believe: The Christian's Creed,* trans. John W. Doberstein and H. George Anderson (Philadelphia: Fortress Press, 1968), p. 52.

causality of the world within God's intention for it, while some feminists compare the relation of God to the world with the relation between our minds and bodies, or, as we saw before, identify the processes of nature with God's activity (in panentheism) or equate God with the life of nature itself (in pantheism). Ian Barbour in *Religion in an Age of Science* does a rather good job of outlining the various metaphysical systems proposed, and I recommend his discussion to you.[15]

Barbour also proposes his own metaphysical explanation of how God works in the natural world, basing it on process theology, and perhaps we need to deal with that metaphysics a little more fully at this point.[16] Barbour really is trying to come to terms with three realities with which the Christian faith certainly must deal in our day — namely, with the scientific, evolutionary view of the universe, with the presence of evil and suffering in the world, and with the phenomenon of human freedom.

Basing his views on Alfred North Whitehead's philosophy, Barbour holds that God the Creator is the primordial ground of all order and novelty in the world. All entities are dependent on him for their existence and for the possibilities that they have. God is omniscient, but he is not omnipotent, though he is always prior in status, and his purposes are not contingent on events in the world. His unchanging and everlasting purpose of good is the achievement within creation of value and harmony among all beings, animate and inanimate alike. All entities are joined together in an interdependent network of relationships, and God is to be thought of as the leader of and participant in their cosmic community. He is not identical with the world and its natural laws, but he never existed apart from the world. Thus, the Christian doctrine of creation *ex nihilo* is rejected, as is the thought that there will be any final kingdom of God. The cosmos is a continuing creation, evolving always toward the future.

15. See Barbour, *Religion in an Age of Science*, pp. 243-59, 267-70.
16. Ibid., pp. 230-41, 260-69.

God has power, but it is never unilateral controlling power that abrogates creaturely power, and his power over nature is limited. According to Barbour, God works in nature, history, religious experience, and Christ primarily by means of his Spirit, but God's action in the Spirit is one cause alongside natural causes and the self-creativity of all entities. All entities have within themselves the ability to respond in self-creativity — that is, they have the potential of newness, although in the case of inanimate objects, their infinitesimal response is largely the maintenance of their own order, with the response of any entity becoming more and more complex the higher one ascends in the level of being. Obviously, human response and potential for freedom and novelty are the most complex of all.

God's work in the world is never coercive, and his grace is never irresistible. He is persuasive love, constantly presenting to all entities and especially to human beings, as the source of all novelty in evolution, new possibilities of greater value and harmony. But God is never the sole cause of any event, and no event can be attributed to God alone. Natural agents or laws and the creature's own self-creativity and freedom always enter in. Indeed, where natural agents or laws are causally efficient, God's ability to lure toward new possibilities is limited, and natural disasters, for example, can be attributed only to the causality of natural laws.

God presents to all entities many new possibilities, and so the response of any entity may be good or bad, leading toward greater harmony and value or away from them. Cosmic history, in its evolution, is a history of trial and error, building always on what is present and pressing always toward the future. Death and suffering are inescapable features within such an evolutionary process, and they have always been present and will always be present, although God is constantly transmuting them into good and envisaging the larger, better pattern into which they may be integrated. God is influenced by the response that the world or all entities make to his persuasion, and he suffers with the world and in it, but he continually acts to present new possibilities for growth and good.

That is, admittedly, a rather sketchy presentation of process theism, and obviously it departs from biblical understandings at many points. But it does illustrate one attempt to explain how God works in his world — to sort out how God is related to the laws of nature and human freedom and the realities of evil and suffering. Christian theology must grapple with all of those questions, and certainly they affect the everyday lives of all people.

I become very nervous, however, when our metaphysical systems depart from what we find in the Scriptures, because it seems to me that the Bible's witness must dictate the shape of our metaphysics and not the other way around. Barbour himself, in developing his system, points out where it is at variance with the Bible, and he admits that "Christianity cannot be identified with any metaphysical system."[17] In fact, he concludes his book with this statement: "Only in worship can we acknowledge the mystery of God and the pretensions of any system of thought claiming to have mapped out God's way."[18] For me that is an acknowledgment of the fact that finally we cannot precisely define *how* God works in the world of nature. His ways are not our ways, and his thoughts are not our thoughts, and as Karl Barth has said, we really are dealing with an entirely different order, unavailable to our science and thought, when we are dealing with the working of God.

In his book entitled *The Medusa and the Snail,* Lewis Thomas gives one example of the uniqueness of God's ways in connection with genetic science:

> We know a lot about DNA, but if our kind of mind had been confronted with the problem of designing a similar replicating molecule, starting from scratch, we'd never have succeeded. We would have made one fatal mistake: our molecule would have been perfect. . . . It would never have occurred to us, thinking as we do, that the thing had to be able to make errors. . . . Each of the mutations that have brought us along represents a random,

17. Ibid., p. 263.
18. Ibid., p. 270.

> totally spontaneous accident, but it is no accident at all that mutations occur; the molecule of DNA was ordained from the beginning to make small mistakes. If we had been doing it, we would have found some way to correct this, and evolution would have been stopped in its tracks.[19]

God's ways are not our ways, and his thoughts are not our thoughts. We therefore need a certain humility in laying out our theological systems, perhaps the same humility that the Wisdom writers of the Old Testament had. They were astute observers of all the processes of nature and of all the ways of human beings, and yet they could say,

> Do you see a man who is wise in his own eyes?
> There is more hope for a fool than for him.
> (Prov. 26:12)

Ultimately we are totally dependent on the transcendent God's self-revelation of his ways and will for our knowledge of his working in the world, and thus the Bible's statements about God's sustaining, providential activity in nature are all finally confessions of faith.

The Positive Dialogue with Science

Joining in that confession and giving voice to the Bible's testimony, we can say certain positive things in dialogues with modern science. Barbour maintains that biblical faith, characterized, for example, in neo-orthodoxy, "can do little with the continuing creation tradition" of modern evolutionary science.[20] But of course it can. There is nothing in the Bible that need cause us to deny the novelty introduced into God's creation by the continuous working of what

19. Thomas, *The Medusa and the Snail* (New York: Viking Press, 1979), pp. 28-29.

20. Barbour, *Religion in an Age of Science*, p. 180.

science calls mutation and natural selection. The story is told of the little girl watching a program about evolution on television. Her mother wanted to interrupt her viewing and interject a religious point of view, to which the little girl responded, "Be quiet, Mother. I want to learn how God did these things." Certainly modern evolutionary theory helps us understand how God did all that he has done and is doing in the natural realm, and we need not neglect its contributions to our understanding. There are some points, however, at which biblical faith should make its own unique contribution to the dialogue with modern science.

First of all, process theism is correct when it says that human freedom must always be considered in our understanding of divine providence. In the Bible, God waits to see what human beings will do, and he not only acts in nature and history but also reacts to human decision making. "See," he says to his people, "I have set before you this day life and good, death and evil" (Deut. 30:15), and he therefore waits to see what choice Israel will make before he reacts to her decision, just as Jesus, in his teachings, constantly sets before his audience and us the necessity of deciding about his person and will in every area of our lives. God takes human decision making and freedom seriously, and he works in nature and history accordingly.

In the Bible's view, therefore, providence has nothing about it of predeterminism, and God's omnipotence does not consist in his control of every human choice and action. Rather, we could say that God's providence and omnipotence in the Bible consist in his ability, despite anything that human beings may do or not do, always faithfully to keep his promises. For example, God promised that he would bring blessing on all the families of the earth through Abraham and his descendants (Gen. 12:3), and Jesus Christ is the fulfillment of that promise (cf. 2 Cor. 1:20; Matt. 1:1; Gal. 3:6-9; et al.). God has promised that every knee shall bow and every tongue confess that Jesus Christ is Lord (Phil. 2:10-11), and God will keep that promise, no matter how sinful human freedom tries to defeat it.

Second, however, in the Bible's view, human freedom and indeed any freedom inherent in nature's ways must always be considered within the framework of universal sin and the Fall. I will take up the subjects of sin and the Fall in the next chapter, but right now it must be noted that we are not so free as we think we are.

Third, evolutionary theory talks about the role of chance in the ongoing creation, of tiny mutations and of chance conditions that spur the progress of evolution or set it back. And some thinkers maintain that is the way God has designed his cosmos, to include chance events within its evolution toward the future. In the passage that I cited from Lewis Thomas, for example, he says that DNA was designed from the beginning to make small mistakes, leading to chance mutations. Perhaps so.

But if we use the Bible's historical narratives as a paradigm, we get a different picture. The Bible does speak of chance. In the book of Ruth, Ruth happens to go to the field of Boaz (2:3), and the story develops from there. In the story of Joseph, Midianite traders happen to pass by, and Joseph is sold to them by his brothers (Gen. 37:28). In the Succession Document of 2 Samuel 6–1 Kings 2, it happens late one afternoon that David sees from his roof a woman bathing (2 Sam. 11:2). Yet, in every one of those narratives, there is a profound sense of God's guidance of the history that takes place. For example, in the Succession Document, God uses the most human of emotions — Amnon's lust, and Absalom's ambition, and Hushai's loyalty — to carry out his purpose of putting Solomon on the Davidic throne (2 Sam. 12:24–1 Kings 2:46), just as in the story of Joseph, God uses the brothers' hatred and treachery and lies to send Joseph ahead into Egypt and thus to save his chosen people in the time of famine (see Gen. 45:4-8). If our understanding of nature's ways grows out of God's revelation in history, we therefore have to at least raise the question if what we call chance in evolution is not rather God's working.

Fourth and finally, in thinking about evolution in connection with God's ways in nature, we have to remember that when our

Lord speaks of the coming kingdom of God, he contradicts the laws of evolution. The meek will inherit the earth, he says (Matt. 5:5), and those who become like children in their dependence on their heavenly Father will inherit the kingdom (Matt. 18:1-4). There is no law of the survival of the fittest in Jesus' teachings. To the contrary, the weak, the oppressed, the suffering, all those who have no other helper but God — these are the ones who receive and will receive God's special care and attention. So contrary to all of those who believe that the kingdom will be the highest point of natural and human evolution, our Lord says to us that the final outcome of nature and history will be not the product of this world but solely the result of God's transcendent making. Perhaps that is the principal point which we need to remember when we try to explain God's ways in the world.

When we confront Jesus' miraculous healings, for example, we are not seeing into the laws of nature, but we are being given a little glimpse into the working of the God who transcends all of nature. Through the person and acts of Jesus Christ, we are granted a glimpse into that final world where there will be no more mourning nor crying nor pain, where the former things will have passed away, where death will have been banished from the earth, and God will have made his new creation (Rev. 21). Such a God cannot be equated with anything that is in the heavens above, or that is on the earth, or that is in the waters surrounding the earth. He can be worshiped only through his Son Jesus Christ as the One who holds the whole cosmos in his hand.

Sample Sermon

I preached this sermon in the summer of 1991 in the cathedral-like "chapel" of Duke University. It takes its major theme from the figure of chaos in the Scriptures.

Contingency, Chaos, and Christ

Scripture Lessons:

2 Corinthians 5:17–6:2

Mark 4:35-41

We live in a contingent universe; that is, it is dependent on something outside of itself for its beginning and its continuing existence. We do not think about that very often, of course. For us, our world and our universe are just givens that are there, and to our minds, they work quite automatically. Everything moves along by natural law, enclosed in a system that is self-sustaining. So it has always been, we feel, and so it will always be. But how did it all get started, and what preserves and holds our universe together?

Our scientists tell us that it is most probable that everything started with one Big Bang. From an infinite concentration of matter, our universe exploded outward to form the stars and the planets and our world as we now know it, and it is still continuing to expand. But there are amazing facts now known to us from that first Big

Bang. As Ian Barbour explains, "If the early rate of expansion had been less by even one part in a thousand billion, the universe would have collapsed again before temperatures had fallen below 10,000 degrees. On the other hand, if the rate had been greater by a part in a million, the universe would have expanded too rapidly for stars and planets to form."[1] Then, too, if the strong nuclear force in the initial explosion had been slightly weaker, we would have had only hydrogen in the universe. If it had been slightly stronger, there would be only helium.[2] What amazing events have taken place to form this good green earth as we know it!

And I suppose we *could* say that all took place by chance. Heaven knows, we cannot prove anything. But as biologist Lewis Thomas once said, "It is absurd to say that a place like this place [like this earth] is absurd"[3] — that is, that it is all the result of chance happenings. Look at the world around us! We are surrounded by billions of different forms of life, each one in its way perfect, and all linked together to form a pulsating, ongoing chain of vital existence and growth and change. Did that all come about by chance?

Some time ago, I had the privilege of holding my one-day-old grandson in my arms, and as I looked at that tiny boy, I was simply overcome with wonder. From the love of our daughter and her husband and one tiny fertilized egg, there now lay in my arms a wiggling human being, with every tiny fingernail formed and every tiny toe in place, with little lips and tongue that knew instinctively how to suck, and little vocal cords that could produce a wail. Was he all the product of chance, dear friends, the automatic conglomeration of atoms? No, I do not think so, any more than I think that each one of you, with your distinctive voice and features and fingerprints, is the product of chance.

1. Barbour, "Creation and Cosmology," in *Cosmos as Creation: Theology and Science in Consonance*, ed. Ted Peters (Nashville: Abingdon Press, 1989), p. 130.

2. Ibid.

3. Lewis, in a commencement address delivered at Stanford University, reported in *The Stanford Observer*, June 1980, p. 2.

Rather, the Bible tells us that you and I and the marvel of this universe that now surrounds us are the result of the creation of God, of God creating order out of chaos. "In the beginning, God . . ." is the confession of faith in Genesis. Everything came forth from God. And so we now walk an earth that he created, and we breathe oxygen that he brought forth, and our hearts pump their steady rhythm by muscles that he made.

In the beginning there was nothing, says the biblical faith — void, darkness, non-life — and the Hebrew mind equated that nothingness with evil and with death, because God is the God of life and good and light and order. But it is very hard to talk about nothing, isn't it? And so the Bible put it in the form of a symbol. It said that nothingness in the beginning before creation was simply chaos — chaotic waters, ocean, sea, with nothing but the Spirit of God blowing over the surface of the waters. And then, Genesis says, God created everything by bringing order into the chaos. God put checks on the chaotic waters and instead of their darkness created light; God bound the chaos and instead of its turbulence brought forth order; in place of the evil of chaos, God created the world good; in place of the death in chaos, God made earth's swarming life and you and me.

And you see, that is not intended by the biblical writers to be a scientific statement. No, it is a confession of faith — a confession that this wondrous universe is not a chance and meaningless happening in the history of the cosmos, but rather that it has behind its existence a Creator God of purpose and love. God intended the universe. God intended you and me. "In the beginning, God. . . ." He created it all in place of chaos.

Well, I tell you all of this because it is the background of the story in Mark that we read for our Gospel lesson this morning. In that story, Jesus and his disciples are crossing the Sea of Galilee. While Jesus is asleep in the stern of the boat, a storm arises and the chaotic waters threaten to swamp the boat and drown them all. And what does Jesus do, according to Mark? He awakes and rebukes the *sea.* He says to the chaotic waters threatening their lives, "Peace! Be still!" And the storm immediately subsides and the disciples ask in wonder, "Who is this, that even wind and *sea* obey him?" Who is this, dear friends, who stills the chaotic waters that threaten all of creation? Well, who was it who put checks and guards on chaos in the beginning? It was God, wasn't it? — the Creator God. And Mark is telling us here in our Gospel lesson that that man in that boat, with all of those frightened disciples, is not just some human prophet from Galilee. He is the Son of God, through whom all things were made, as the New Testament says elsewhere. And his power is the power of the Creator who in the beginning called forth our universe.

Do you remember, however, the question that the frightened disciples asked Jesus before he stilled the storm? "Lord," they shouted at him over the sound of the wind, as they woke him up, "do you not care if we perish?" And though Jesus rebuked his disciples for their lack of faith, it is clear that he cared and still cares very much.

As some of you know, our scientists tell us that it is impossible to determine how the electrons in this universe are going to act. If you know the position of an electron, you cannot calculate its velocity; but if you know the velocity of its movement, you cannot tell exactly where it is. And when I hear all of that, my naive imagination starts to run wild. Great Scott, I think to myself, what holds everything together? What if everything just starts to rearrange itself? What if there are no constants? What if the electrons in the roof of this building suddenly forget where they are going? What if, as Yeats said, "things fall apart; the center cannot hold"? What if?

Ah, but God, you see — the Father and the Son and the Holy Spirit — conquered the chaos in the beginning, and by his faithful care he still holds it in check. And so not only the beginning but now even the very structure of our world is dependent on his faithfulness. And because he cares for each one of us, "seedtime and harvest, cold and heat, summer and winter, day and night, shall not cease." And the stars will all follow their accustomed orbits, and the flowers will still bloom in Duke Gardens. As G. K.

Chesterton once poetically expressed it, "The sun doesn't rise by natural law; it rises because God says, 'Get up and do it again.'" Or let's put it in the words of Colossians: All things hold together in Christ (1:17). He cares for us. He does not wish us to perish. And so he gives us this wondrous world to live in, and then he preserves and sustains its order and light and life, day and night without ceasing.

The Bible uses our figure of chaos in other ways, however. Not only does it talk about God holding chaos in check to create and sustain our universe, but it also uses the figure of chaos to symbolize the disorder in our personal and public lives.

What is chaos, according to the Scriptures? In the book of Job, it symbolizes the void of meaninglessness over which Job's life dangles in his suffering; or it is the pathless waste through which the nations of the world wander in their affairs, without wisdom and guidance. In the prophets, chaos is a symbol of the powerlessness and delusion of those who worship false gods; or it is a figure of life that brings no result, of life lived apart from all truth and purpose.

And I think we all sometimes know those kinds of chaos in our lives, do we not — when our days and labors make no sense, and our existence seems like just one big evil joke? I once drove behind a young woman in a red convertible who had that one word on her bumper sticker — *chaos* — and I was not sure if that was the name of a new rock group or her personal confession about her life — that it was chaos.

But certainly we know what the word means at those times when everything seems to fall apart — shall we say when the divorce decree becomes final and our life seems nothing but failure, or perhaps when we have made a whole string of bad decisions, or when our kids are making theirs? Or is it two weeks after the funeral when we cannot seem to get organized and loneliness sits in our living room? Chaos. How right the Bible is when it says that without God, the chaos can come again. It comes time and again into our troubled lives.

But in the midst of those times, I hope you will remember our

Gospel lesson: over against the chaos that threatens us so often, there is that figure in that boat on the Sea of Galilee who says to the chaotic waves and storm, "Peace! Be still!" There is God, the Father and the Son and the Spirit, who conquered the chaos when he created our world and who can conquer it still.

Indeed, says our Epistle lesson, God in Christ can conquer all the forces of chaos daily. He can even make of our jumbled lives brand-new creations. "If any one is in Christ, [that person] is a new creation; the old has passed away, behold, the new has come" (2 Cor. 5:17). In Christ there can be once again goodness and order, light and life, just as there was at the original creation of the world, when God said, "Let it be," and all the morning stars sang together.

A story is told of the great eighteenth-century Lutheran scholar Johann Albrecht Bengel, to whom we owe the foundations of modern New Testament textual criticism. Bengel was a professor in charge of a theological training school at Denkendorff, Germany. One day he fell seriously ill, and he sent for a theological student at the school to give him a word of consolation. But the youth replied, "Sir, I am but a pupil, a mere learner; I don't know what to say to a great teacher like *you*." "What," said Bengel, "a divinity student, and not able to communicate a word of scriptural comfort?" whereupon the flustered student managed to stutter out a biblical sentence: "The blood of Jesus Christ, the Son of God, cleanses us from all sin." "Ah," sighed Bengel, "that is the very word I want. It is quite enough."

"Lord, do you not care if we perish?" O yes, good Christians, he cares desperately that we not be overwhelmed and done to death by darkness and evil and the terrible failures and disorders of our lives. And so God was in Christ, reconciling the world to himself, not counting our trespasses against us but taking them all, all upon himself, and nailing them to a cross, and then burying them, defeating them, rising triumphant over them, and giving you and me a new beginning, as if we were brand-new creations of our loving Creator God.

And so what is there to fear, good Christians? What is there to fear if we trust him? In the words of the Psalmist,

> God is our refuge and strength,
> a very present help in trouble.
> Therefore we will not fear though the earth should change,
> though the mountains shake in the heart of the *sea.*
> (46:1-2, my emphasis)

In other words, though all chaos — the chaotic waters — threaten to overwhelm and destroy us.

What is there to fear? Nothing at all, is there? Because we have a God who made the world in the beginning, and who endowed it with life and light and order and goodness. Who now maintains the stars in their courses and sends his rain to water the earth. Who feeds the thrush that sings in the willow tree and clothes the lilies of the field in a glory exceeding Solomon's. Who gives the work of day and the rest of night, and brings forth each new generation. Who numbers the very hairs on our heads and knows when one sparrow falls to earth.

And the same faithful God in Christ, who created it all in the beginning and who sustains it all by his care, now says to the chaotic storms in our lives, "Peace! Be still!" And he pours out his love upon us from a cross and rises triumphant over all our evil. And he can make us new creations by his love because he does not wish us to perish.

No, friends, there is nothing to fear — nothing at all, if we trust him. Amen.

CHAPTER 6

The Dark Shadow

Modern science is built on the assumption of the rationality of the cosmos and on the ability of the human mind to comprehend that rationality. As Albert Einstein once said, "A conviction, akin to religious feeling, of the rationality or intelligibility of the world lies behind all scientific work of a high order."[1] Indeed, for Einstein, God was intimately connected with the orderly structure of the universe, and Einstein was sure that the uncertainties and indeterminacies of quantum physics reflected merely temporary human ignorance.[2] "God does not play dice," he said,[3] a quote that reveals the underlying presupposition of his epistemology.

As we have seen, other thinkers and theologians acknowledge the presence of chance, of indeterminacy, and of disruptive and what might be called evil events in the process of the evolution of the world. For example, Annie Dillard, in pages of evocative and affective prose-poetry, wonders why creatures can lay millions of eggs and have only a few of them survive. It's like making nine thousand railroad engines, she writes, each perfect in every detail,

1. Einstein, *Ideas and Opinions* (London: Souvenir Press, 1973), p. 262.

2. Ian Barbour, *Religion in an Age of Science*, the Gifford Lectures, vol. 1 (San Francisco: Harper & Row, 1990), p. 142.

3. Einstein, quoted in ibid., p. 102.

and then assigning them to the same stretch of track with no one manning the switches. "The engines crash, collide, derail, jump, jam, burn," she says, and "at the end of the massacre you have three engines, which is what the run could support in the first place. . . . It's a hell of a way to run a railroad," she points out, and the systems of evolution seem no better.[4]

Yet for all of that seeming chaos built into the evolutionary system, many are convinced that the cosmos is orderly and rational, that the fundamental structure of the natural world is both simple and beautiful, and that finally there lies before modern physics a unified field system that will encompass the basic laws of the universe in one simple and all-inclusive equation. Combine that belief in the order and intelligibility of the world with religious faith, and you get an optimistic statement such as this from Philip Hefner: "The world about us is . . . a fundamentally friendly home for us. The ecosystem is benevolent and reliable. It cannot be otherwise if it has proceeded originally from God's creative intention and continues to be sustained by the will of God."[5]

Certainly that was the theological outlook of the Wisdom theologians of the Old Testament. God made all things wisely and well, in their view, and there was no reason to be afraid (Ps. 104:24; Prov. 3:19-20). The Creator had set certain orders into both the natural and the human worlds — customary ways in which human beings and natural phenomena behaved — and if one was wise and learned to live in accordance with those orders, one could live the good life.

Today we can still hold that belief. There are natural orders that must be obeyed in order to live. Rivers overflow their banks, and so if you are wise, you do not build your houses on a river floodplain, as Wilkes-Barre, Pennsylvania, learned so well during Hurricane Agnes. Continental plates collide and cause earth-

4. Dillard, *Pilgrim at Tinker Creek* (New York: Bantam Books, 1975), pp. 178-79.

5. Hefner, "The Evolution of the Created Co-Creator," in *Cosmos as Creation: Theology and Science in Consonance*, ed. Ted Peters (Nashville: Abingdon Press, 1989), p. 226.

quakes, and so wise persons do not erect cities and nuclear power plants over earthquake faults — a lesson that we still apparently have not learned. Similarly, in the ethical realm, my own mother early impressed upon me the fact that God had established certain moral orders in human life, which, if learned and heeded, led to happy living. A marriage does not prosper, for example, when one of the partners commits adultery. We live daily on the assumption of the natural and moral order of the universe.

Some, of course, are naive and believe that their world is so orderly that education then is the key to making a perfect society. Or that all our difficulties will be solved by proper economics, as in Marxism, or proper government, as in socialism, or proper environments for children, as in liberal psychological theory. As T. S. Eliot once remarked, we keep tinkering with the system so that none of us will have to be good. Just perfect the system, and everything will be fine. For example, get rid of sexism, proclaim the feminist ideologues, and the solution of every other problem will follow.

The Corruption of Creation

The Bible, that most realistic of books, knows that the world is not so orderly as we would like to believe and that at the heart of both nature and history there is some deep corruption. Job and Ecclesiastes and some of the Psalmists called into question the optimism of Wisdom theology, and indeed, that theology itself set boundaries on human understanding of the universe. Human beings are wondrous creatures, it said, and they have wondrous technological and intellectual powers,

> but where shall wisdom be found?
>   And where is the place of understanding?
> Mortals do not know the way to it,
>   and it is not found in the land of the living.
>
> (Job 28:12-13, NRSV)

There is no way to read the way to a perfect order from the orderliness and rationality of the universe, for that universe itself participates in some awful disorder and irrationality. Listen again to Annie Dillard as she tells us about parasites:

> Parasitic insects comprise ten percent of all known animal species. How can this be understood? Certainly we give our infants the wrong idea about their fellow creatures in the world. Teddy bears should come with tiny stuffed bear-lice; ten percent of all baby bibs and rattles should be adorned with colorful blowflies, maggots, and screw-worms. . . . This itch, this gasp in the lung, this coiled worm in the gut, hatching egg in the sinew, warblehole in the hide — is a sort of rent, paid by all creatures who live in the real world with us now. . . . Chomp. It is the thorn in the flesh of the world, another sign if any be needed, that the world is actual and fringed, pierced here and there, and through and through, with the toothed conditions of time and the mysterious, coiled spring of death.[6]

The world is not so orderly as we would like to believe.

Our realistic Bible has many ways of expressing that. It maintains in Genesis 9 that some dark shadow of human beings now falls over all the earth:

> The fear of you and the dread of you shall be upon every beast of the earth, and upon every bird of the air, upon everything that creeps on the ground and all the fish of the sea; into your hand they are delivered. Every moving thing that lives shall be food for you; and as I gave you the green plants, I give you everything. (vv. 2-3)

We cast a dark shadow upon every one of earth's creatures because we can kill them and we can eat them.[7] But whether worm in the

6. Dillard, *Pilgrim at Tinker Creek,* pp. 238-40.

7. In an important article in French entitled "Creation et fondation de la loi en Gn 1,1–2,4" (*La Creatio dans l'orient ancien,* ed. F. Blanquart [Paris: Les

gut or bear in the forest or shark in the ocean, they can also kill and eat us, can't they? Chomp. And so throughout the pages of the Old Testament, there is pictured an antagonism between human beings and animals. In 1 Samuel, David, in his life as a shepherd, had to be delivered from the paws of the lion and the bear (17:37). In the books of Kings, dogs lick up the blood of murderous Ahab (1 Kings 21:19; 22:38) and of Jezebel (2 Kings 9:10, 36). In 2 Kings 2:24, two she-bears come out of the woods to devour the boys who make fun of Elisha, just as a lion kills the disobedient prophet in 1 Kings 13:24 (cf. 1 Kings 20:36).

In the world of most of the Old Testament, nature is not benign or benevolent but threatening and terrifying. Therefore, the one "who dwells in the shelter of the Most High,/who abides in the shadow of the Almighty," must be reassured of God's protection from the terrors of nature:

> You will tread on the lion and the adder,
> the young lion and the serpent you will trample under foot.
> (Ps. 91:1, 13)

In Deuteronomy 7:22, Israel is even warned not to drive out the other nations too quickly as she enters the promised land, lest the wild beasts become too numerous for her to defend herself against them.

In the light of this antagonism of nature, the Gospel according to Mark surprises us at the end of the story of the temptation of Jesus in the wilderness with the notice that Jesus "was with the wild beasts; and the angels ministered to him" (1:13), just as much earlier 1 Kings surprised us with the notice that the ravens fur-

---

Editions du Cerf, 1987], pp. 139-82), P. Beauchamp has argued that Genesis 9:1-7 implies an increase in human domination over the animals, which now fear human beings. In Genesis 1:26-30, humanity, made in the image of God, exercised its dominion by tenderness toward other creatures. In Genesis 9:1-7, the image is marred, the domination has become warlike, and human beings kill not only animals but each other as well.

nished Elijah with bread and meat in the morning and the evening (17:6). There is something different about Elijah and Jesus, the writers are telling us, for otherwise the antagonism of nature can be an instrument of God's judgment:

> I will appoint over them four kinds of destroyers, says the Lord: the sword to slay, the dogs to tear, and the birds of the air and the beasts of the earth to devour and destroy. (Jer. 15:3)

Jeremiah and Ezekiel repeatedly see in the threat of the natural world the means of God's judgment:

> But they all alike had broken the yoke,
> they had burst the bonds.
> Therefore a lion from the forest shall slay them,
> a wolf from the desert shall destroy them.
> A leopard is watching against their cities,
> every one who goes out of them shall be torn in pieces.
> (Jer. 5:5-6; cf. 12:9)

> "For behold, I am sending among you serpents,
> adders which cannot be charmed,
> and they shall bite you," says the Lord.
> (Jer. 8:17; cf. Deut. 32:24)

> I will send famine and wild beasts against you, and they will rob you of your children. (Ezek. 5:17; cf. 14:15; 39:17)

Further, the antagonism of nature over against human beings is so taken for granted that God in his wrathful judgment can repeatedly compare himself to a devouring lion (Hos. 5:14; Jer. 25:38) or to a bear robbed of her cubs (Hos. 13:7-8). Or, in a startling figure, the Lord compares himself to a moth eating up the fabric of our lives (Hos. 5:12; Ps. 39:11; cf. Isa. 50:9; 51:8). Or in Hosea 5:12 he even likens himself to what we now know are the bacteria of dry rot that undermine our foundations.

In the thought of much of the Bible, the world of nature is

no peaceable kingdom. Rather, the people of God are continually threatened, not only by beasts and serpents but also by fire and lightning (Job 1:16; cf. Num. 11:1), destroying wind (Job 1:19; Ps. 48:7; Jer. 4:11-12), disease and plagues and scabrous growths (Exod. 32:35; 2 Sam. 12:14-15; 24:15; 2 Kings 15:5; 2 Chron. 21:18; Isa. 3:17), drought and famine and locusts (Jer. 14:1-10; 42:16; 2 Sam. 21:1; Isa. 14:30; Amos 7:1), and pestilence and tumors (1 Sam. 5:6; Num. 14:12; 1 Chron. 21:14), all of which can be instruments of the wrath of the Lord who controls them.

This is not to say that every natural disaster which happens in our day should be viewed as a judgment from God. There are times in the Bible when a natural disaster takes place unaccompanied by any mention of God's use of it in judgment (e.g., Gen. 12:10; 1 Kings 19:11-12). God has indeed set orders and processes into the natural world, which, if we defy them, lead us to bring disaster upon our own heads. Certainly too, when other people suffer a natural catastrophe, we cannot point a finger at them and declare that they are suffering for their sin. When we suffer natural calamity, it does seem wise, however, in the light of a passage such as Amos 4:6-10, to ask if God is trying to tell us something, to urge upon us repentance, or to turn our lives in another direction. The Lord of nature can use nature's forces in his work of discipline and judgment.

Indeed, according to Hosea, God can prevent in Israel conceptions and pregnancies and births, giving instead miscarrying wombs and dry breasts (9:11-12). So Solomon, in his prayer at the dedication of the temple, prays in this manner:

> When heaven is shut up and there is no rain because they have sinned against thee, if they pray toward this place, . . . then hear thou in heaven . . . and grant rain upon thy land. . . . If there is famine in the land, if there is pestilence or blight or mildew or locust or caterpillar; . . . whatever plague, whatever sickness there is; whatever prayer, whatever supplication is made by any man or by all thy people Israel . . . then hear thou in heaven thy dwelling place, and forgive, and act. (1 Kings 8:35-39)

God controls the ways of nature and uses them in his judgment on his people, but the point is that in his judgment he uses that which is at hand. He uses the antagonism of the natural world toward human beings — those deep and fundamental corruptions that have put nature out of joint and made it possible for it to be a power for evil rather than for good. Moth and rust consume, says the Lord. They chomp away. So do not lay up treasures for yourselves that can fall victim to that corruption (Matt. 6:19-20). Dark powers now are loose in our world, in ourselves, and in the whole cosmos around us. The Bible knows that, and in that knowing, it is a very realistic book.

Sin, the Root of Corruption

Where did this corruption of the universe come from? We all know the answer — it came from us. In Pogo's language, "We have met the enemy, and he is us." God made the world "very good," with all things beautiful and orderly, and the dark shadow laid upon the face of the earth is the shadow of sinful humankind.

Loren Eiseley wrote of an experience he once had when he was a child. After removing a cover from an old well, he peered down along a shaft of sunlight into the well's dark and dank depths. Some twenty feet down there was a rusty pipe projecting across the well space, he says, and he saw suddenly scurrying along that pipe into the darkness a spidery thing of hair and many legs. Shivering and horrified, he quickly set the rotting boards covering the well back into place. "Something that did not love the sun was down there," he wrote, "something that could walk through total darkness upon slender footholds over evil waters, something that had come down there by preference from above."[8] And that's the way it is with life. Scientists used to think that human life evolved from the primal

8. Eiseley, *The Immense Journey* (New York: Random House–Vintage Books, 1946), pp. 37-38.

ooze at the bottom of the sea. But after countless investigations, they know better now. Human life came into being on this planet when there was air and light and green. And if we have descended into some abyss of darkness, we have worked our way down. God created life good; we turned it into evil. As Jesus told us, we have loved the darkness rather than the light (John 3:19).

The Bible tells the story of that corrupted and corrupting love in Genesis 3, of course — that chapter which is meant to be the story of the way we all have walked in our relationship with God. We have previously discussed, in Chapters 3 and 4 of this book, what we were meant to be and how. Genesis 3 now tells us what we have become — rebels in the kingdom of God, subversives of his purposes, refusing to acknowledge our creaturely limits and attempting to be our own gods and goddesses. But Genesis also tells us what effect that sin has had on the world of nature. It has marred and distorted every one of God's good gifts.

The wondrous natural desire of the sexes for one another that leads to the love of marriage and home and family now has been blemished with fear of one another and shame (cf. Gen. 3:7), so that healthy desire can be replaced by lust and the will to power over another (cf. 1 Thess. 4:3-5). Males or females are turned into objects to be conquered (cf. Gen. 3:16). Marriage becomes just a restriction to be scorned in the pursuit of permissiveness. Sex becomes the dirty object of pornography, rape, and incest, and woman an object to be admired for the size of her mammary glands.

The love and good fellowship and sharing that naturally bind families together are marred with jealousy and deceit and hatred, and siblings become rivals for favor or money or power, until personalities are warped and anger dominates and breaks up households and sometimes even leads to murder (cf. Gen. 4:1-16; chap. 27).

The beauty of the world around us falls victim to chain saw and bulldozer, pesticides and war, pollution and desecration — everywhere gum wrappers, cigarette butts, and scrawled and filthy graffiti — until we no longer know what is lovely and pure and can call junk and obscenity art.

The gift of daily bread becomes a problem for dieters and anorectics and bulimics, or we die early from overweight; meanwhile, two-thirds of the world's children go to bed hungry every night, and thousands die from malnutrition.

The good gift of daily work is turned into drudgery, boredom, frustration, sometimes its only object to earn enough to buy a $150 pair of sneakers. How often we find that our toil and sweat have produced only the thorns and thistles of life (Gen. 3:18), when businesses become the scenes of scrambles for power, for prestige, for sources of conspicuous consumption, and human beings who labor in them are valued only for what they produce.

Communities and nations no longer can live in peace (cf. Gen. 4:23-24; 11:1-9), so police forces and prisons and armies must grow ever larger. Violence walks our streets at night and loneliness sits in our living rooms, while we invent ever better security systems to guard ourselves from our neighbors.

Everywhere, everywhere around us we sense the hint, the risk, the "mysterious, coiled spring of death," to use Dillard's phrase. And the abundant life that God intended for us all in the beginning is marred and distorted. Listen to Jeremiah's description of us, comparing us to beasts in what we have become:

> How can you say, "I am not defiled . . ."?
> Look at your way in the valley;
>   know what you have done —
> a restive young camel interlacing her tracks,
>   a wild ass used to the wilderness,
> in her heat sniffing the wind!
>   Who can restrain her lust?
>
> (2:23-24)

Is that an unfair picture of the lusts, the power plays, the violence, the ugliness that we have introduced into our world? We want to be our own deities, don't we? We want to do without God in the world. And in that lust for ultimate status, security, and power (cf. Gen. 11:1-9), we often indeed become beasts.

But the final gift of God that we lose, says Genesis, is life itself. In our attempts to be divine, our mortality is hurled back at us by our Creator. We are expelled from the garden, driven far from the tree of life, because dust we are and to dust we shall return — to the meaningless dark, the futile *finis,* the void, the nothing, the grave (Gen. 3:19, 22-24).

The profound and poignant note that Genesis inserts in this story of our lives, however, is that one sentence in Genesis 3:17, "Cursed is the ground because of you," a curse that re-echoes throughout the rest of the Bible (cf. Gen. 4:11-12), until Paul gives confirmation of it once again in his epistle to the Romans: "We know that the whole creation has been groaning in travail together until now" (8:22). Nothing is "natural" anymore. That is, nothing is as God made it. Our scientists are not studying a "natural" world; they are studying an unnatural one — a cosmos distorted and groaning in travail because of human sin. Paul Santmire has maintained that there is no thought of a "cosmic fall" in the Bible,[9] but that contradicts what we find in the writings of Paul and of the prophets, as we shall see. In the Bible's view, our rebellion, our attempt to live without God, has corrupted the universe around us so that everything is out of joint and not as God intended. The poet Gerard Manley Hopkins pictured that disruption in "God's Grandeur":

> Generations have trod, have trod, have trod;
> And all is seared with trade; bleared, smeared with toil;
> And wears man's smudge and shares man's smell: the soil
> Is bare now, nor can foot feel, being shod.[10]

But the prophets of the Old Testament especially are the ones who clearly see the connection between our sin and nature's ruin:

9. Santmire, "The Future of the Cosmos and the Renewal of the Church's Life with Nature," in *Cosmos as Creation*, p. 275.

10. Hopkins, "God's Grandeur," in *Poems and Prose,* selected and edited by W. H. Gardner (New York: Penguin Books, 1953), p. 27, ll. 5-8.

How long will the land mourn,
 and the grass of every field wither?
For the wickedness of those who dwell in it
 the beasts and the birds are swept away.
(Jer. 12:4; cf. 3:3, 24; 9:10-13; 23:10)

There is no faithfulness or kindness,
 and no knowledge of God in the land;
there is swearing, lying, killing, stealing, and committing adultery;
 they break all bounds and murder follows murder.
Therefore the land mourns,
 and all who dwell in it languish,
and also the beasts of the field,
 and the birds of the air;
 and even the fish of the sea are taken away.
(Hos. 4:1-3)

The earth mourns and withers,
 the world languishes and withers;
 the heavens languish together with the earth.
The earth lies polluted
 under its inhabitants;
for they have transgressed the laws,
 violated the statutes,
 broken the everlasting covenant.
(Isa. 24:4-5, in an eschatological passage; cf. 33:7-9)

If we ask how we see the ruin of nature by our sin in our day, then of course our ecological crisis comes to mind. But the issue is deeper than that, in the biblical view, so that all of the processes and materials of nature participate in some awful corruption. It may be, therefore, that when natural calamities come upon us, God is simply allowing the effects of our sin that has ruined nature to return upon our own heads, as the Bible would phrase it (cf. 1 Kings 8:32; Rom. 1:24, 26).

In this connection, I also cannot help but think of the notice that appeared in newspapers in November of 1989, after the Berlin Wall dividing East and West Germany was dismantled. Thousands of dogs which had guarded that wall against escapees from the East had to be put to death, because they could no longer be trained to be peaceful pets — our sin corrupted their nature. Or I think of the porpoises that are used by the military to attach explosives to the sides of enemy ships. Our violence corrupts the intelligence and play of peaceful porpoises. Or I think of miscarriages, birth defects, genetics gone haywire. Could it be that our sin has corrupted even our genes, our natural selves at their deepest level? Gays and lesbians, defending their life-style these days, often claim that God made them homosexual and that therefore their sexual practices are acceptable. But could it be that God did not intend for anyone to be born homosexual any more than he intended for anyone to be born with Down's syndrome?

Similarly, I also think that we at least have to ask if some of the waste we see in the process of evolution and some of what we call chance, as well as creatures like the awful parasites pictured by Annie Dillard, are not the result of the distortions we have introduced into the natural world. We cannot answer the question, but we do at least know that a vast corruption gnaws at the vitals of our universe, affecting every atom, every gene, every seed in every being. As the ancient prayer has it, "We have done those things which we ought not to have done, and there is no health in us."

Moreover, in the Bible's view, the distortion in the universe, sin, has taken on a power of its own. For the biblical writers sin is not a subjective act on the part of an individual but an objective force to which human beings and the world fall captive. We find this already in the writings of the prophets:

> Their deeds do not permit them
> to return to their God.

> For the spirit of harlotry is within them,
> and they know not the Lord.
>
> (Hos. 5:4)

An evil has invaded Israel's life and holds her captive, Hosea is saying, just as in the oracles of Jeremiah, Judah is totally unable to mend her ways:

> Can the Ethiopian change his skin
> or the leopard his spots?
> Then also you can do good
> who are accustomed to do evil.
>
> (13:23)

Thus, in both Jeremiah and Ezekiel, the only cure for Israel is a thoroughgoing transformation of her being by the gift of a new heart and spirit, so that God himself gives the power to do the good that Israel has no ability in herself to do:

> A new heart I will give you, and a new spirit I will put within you; and I will take out of your flesh the heart of stone and give you a heart of flesh. And I will put my spirit within you, and cause you to walk in my statutes and be careful to observe my ordinances. (Ezek. 36:26-27; cf. Jer. 31:31-34)

But Paul, above all other biblical writers, knows the objective power of sin that makes it impossible for the unbeliever to do what he or she ought to do (Rom. 7:17-24), that corrupts mind (Rom. 12:1-2) and conscience (Rom. 9:1-2), that turns the good and just law into an instrument of death (Rom. 7:7-12), that consigns all persons to sin's wages of death (Rom. 5:12; 6:23), and that corrupts the entire creation (Rom. 8:22). Thus the writer of Ephesians, in the tradition of Pauline theology, can say that "we are not contending against flesh and blood, but against the principalities, against the powers, against the world rulers of this present darkness, against the spiritual hosts of wickedness in the heavenly places," and it is only the power of God in Jesus Christ, who created the world in the first place and constantly rules over it, which can overcome that objective power of evil which has invaded our universe (Eph. 6:12-17; cf. 1:21; 2:2; 3:10; John 12:31; Acts 26:18).

In the light of that, it is very clear why moralistic preaching does no good, for those who have been captured by the objective power of sin have no possibility in themselves to free themselves from that power, and only the Word of the cross can defeat those "spiritual hosts of wickedness" that hold them captive.

Because the whole universe is subject to the corrupting power of sin, it is also clear that any romantic notion about a human return to nature and its supposed innocence in order to find the good life is nonsense. Nature no longer is innocent, and doing just "what comes naturally" simply binds us to a world of corruption, despite Hollywood's glorification of the Blue Lagoon and Tarzan of the Apes. We need to change some of our common expressions that assume the goodness of nature: "Boys will be boys"; "That's just human nature"; "It's only natural to act or think that way." No, nothing is natural anymore. Everything has become unnatural, or as Paul would say, apart from God in Christ, we are all slaves of sin (Rom. 6:16-17).

Similarly, any radical environmentalist notion that all we have to do to solve our ecological crisis is to leave nature totally unspoiled ignores the fact that nature and its processes are already spoiled. And any ideological crusade which imagines that it will construct an ideal society from the stuff and dreams of this world overlooks the truth that the stuff and dreams of this world have all now been twisted and tinged by a nightmare called the Fall. The cosmos, in all its parts and processes, is not what God intended it to be, and daily we and all of the natural world suffer the evil effects of that distortion.

Suffering and Death as Unnatural

Throughout the Bible, therefore, sickness, pain, suffering, and death are seen as unnatural intrusions into our world — evil consequences perpetrated upon God's good creation by human rebellion against him. The Bible has several ways of expressing that.

First of all, in the Holiness Code of Leviticus 17–26, we find the stipulation, which seems terribly unfair to us, that no one with a physical infirmity or blemish of any kind may be allowed to be a priest, offering sacrifices before the altar (21:16-24), just as in 2 Samuel 5:8, David quotes the popular proverb to the effect that the blind and lame cannot enter the temple. From our perspective, that is terrible discrimination, but the reasoning behind it is that physical infirmities are corruptions of a world intended by God to be whole, and such corruption has no place in the sphere of the holy. How revolutionary it is, therefore, when our Lord tells us that the poor and maimed and blind and lame are those who will enter the kingdom (Luke 14:21-24), and when in Matthew 21:14, the blind and the lame are precisely those whom Jesus heals *in the temple,* much to the indignation of the chief priests and scribes (v. 15). Nevertheless, behind the Old Testament's reasoning is the thought that sickness and infirmities are unnatural intrusions in the good world God has created.

By the same token, the Holiness Code prescribes that all offerings to God must be unblemished (Lev. 22:17-25), just as the Passover lamb must have no bone of it broken (Exod. 12:46; Num. 9:12), and that law is quoted again in John 19:36 in connection with Jesus' crucifixion. In addition, there are elaborate laws in the Old Testament protecting against contamination by human or animal dead (Lev. 11:29-40; 21:11; Num. 5:2; 6:6; et al.), for death is a corruption not intended by the God of life.

The clearest indications of the intrusive nature of sickness, pain, disease, and death are of course the healings and the restorations to life done by prophets in the Old Testament, especially Elijah and Elisha, and then finally by our Lord in the New. "Go and tell John what you have seen and heard," Jesus tells the

Baptist's disciples: "the blind receive their sight, the lame walk, lepers are cleansed, and the deaf hear, the dead are raised up, the poor have good news preached to them" (Luke 7:22). The infirmities and mortality that afflict human life are not intended by God but are the blot of our sin upon the earth, and when the Son of God walks the earth, he restores human life to its original and intended wholeness.

Perhaps that is expressed most clearly in the story of Jesus' healing of the paralytic in Mark 2:1-12 (cf. John 5:10-15), for Jesus first deals not with the paralysis of the sufferer but with the heart of the problem. "My son," he says to the man, "your sins are forgiven" (Mark 2:5), and sin's captivity and corruption of the man's life are thereby overcome.

Similarly, the epistle of James urges prayer in faith for the sick "in the name of the Lord" (5:14), just as Paul is sure that improper and unfaithful participation in the Lord's Supper brings with it weakness and illness and death (1 Cor. 11:29-30). Sin is the awful corruption that lies like a blanket upon the face of the earth and distorts its processes.

There is one exception to this biblical understanding, and that is found in Exodus 4:11. In that verse the Lord asks Moses, "Who has made man's mouth? Who makes him dumb, or deaf, or seeing, or blind? Is it not I, the Lord?" All these questions seem to imply that God has created the handicapped that way, but that is an isolated text, it seems to me, which is overwhelmed by evidence to the contrary.

The biblical views of sickness, pain, and death raise all sorts of questions, to be sure. Is predation in the animal world unintended by God and part of the corruption caused by sin, or is the food chain involving all creatures a natural and good part of creation? The Bible gives no unambiguous answer. On the one hand, in Psalm 104, predation is a natural order set up by the Lord himself (vv. 21, 27). On the other, the prophetic promise of the kingdom of God portrays the wolf dwelling with the lamb, the leopard lying down with the kid, the cow and the bear feeding alike, and the lion eating straw like the ox (Isa. 11:6-7; 65:25). "They shall not hurt or destroy/in all my holy mountain" is the promise (Isa. 11:9; 65:25). So when God creates a new heaven and a new earth, will the food chain as we know it be transformed?

Most puzzling is the place of death. Both Paul and the Fourth Gospel tell us that the decisive victory over death has been won in the cross and resurrection of Jesus Christ (John 11:25-26; 1 Cor. 15), although human beings still die in this world, as the end to their existence. But according to Paul, at the end all death will be done away: "The last enemy to be destroyed is death" (1 Cor. 15:26) — just as Revelation 21 states that "death shall be no more" (v. 4). Is death always to be seen then as the unnatural product of our universal sin? And does that apply also to the animal world and to the cycle of life and death in nature? Evolution, in our scientific thought, involves the ongoing process of coming into existence and of passing away, and many scientists consider that such natural progression will last indefinitely, or at least until the law of entropy finally brings our universe to an end. But will all nature and history reach a static state of finality in which death is no more? Or rather, will this universe as we know it be replaced by a new creation unlike this one in which we live?

There are a lot of questions that we cannot answer definitively on the basis of the Bible's testimony. But what we can do is finally to examine the biblical promises that are held out before us, and that we will do in our final chapter dealing with the Bible's eschatology.

Continuing Grace

Right now, however, let us end this chapter with a celebration of the grace of God. According to the Bible, you and I live in a spoiled universe, a universe corrupted in all its parts by our sinful attempts to be our own gods and goddesses. And yet there is a marvelous common grace that sustains the life of nature and humans and preserves order from giving way to chaos. As Gerard Manley Hopkins says in the last several lines of "God's Grandeur," despite all of our sinful distortion of the earth,

> nature is never spent;
> There lives the dearest freshness deep down things;
> And though the last lights off the black West went
> Oh, morning, at the brown brink eastward, springs —
> Because the Holy Ghost over the bent
> World broods with warm breast and with ah! bright wings.[11]

Or let's put it in the words of Jesus: God "makes his sun rise on the evil and on the good, and sends rain on the just and on the unjust" (Matt. 5:45). God still faithfully preserves the round of the seasons, so that "seedtime and harvest, cold and heat, summer and winter, day and night" do not cease (Gen. 8:22). He keeps the stars in their orbits and whirls electrons about their nuclei, so that scientists can study and measure and sometimes predict and count on some unchanging patterns in nature. God accommodates living creatures to one another, so that life multiplies and is preserved. He brings forth children to gladden our lives and binds families together in caring and sharing.

Indeed, God gives and sustains even the smallest manifestations of his grace: the faithfulness and protection of our family dog; the beauty of daisies along the roadside; the glories of trees and clouds, of falling water and snow; the warmth of fire; and the rest of sleep that blesses every night. When our hearts are troubled, a thrush still sings outside in the evergreen. And when the death of a loved one terribly deprives and pains us, the comfort of tears and friends gives us courage and helps fill the void. A common grace blesses our lives and lightens the darkness of the shadow we have cast on earth, and for all our evil, we know moments of joy and peace and quiet assurance and goodness.

God preserves his order despite our chaos. Whether we be

11. Ibid., ll. 9-14.

good or bad, believing or unbelieving, moral or immoral, a magnificent mercy encompasses us and cares for us and preserves our lives and our world. And surely that is something of what Colossians means when it says that all things hold together in Christ (1:17). For whether we know Christ or not, God through his love in Jesus Christ preserves our universe and daily lavishes on us his benefits:

> O the depth of the riches and wisdom and knowledge of God! How unsearchable are his judgments and how inscrutable his ways! . . . For from him and through him and to him are all things. To him be glory for ever. Amen. (Rom. 11:33, 36)

Sample Meditation

This brief chapel meditation sets forth, in sermonic form, God's continuing grace despite our sin, the thought that concluded the preceding chapter. It therefore seemed appropriate to include it here.

Season's Meaning

Scripture Lessons:

Genesis 6:5-8; 8:20-22

Romans 5:6-11

Richmond is a beautiful city, and it is difficult to say at what season it is the most beautiful — whether in the spring, when the sight of azaleas and dogwood causes us to catch our breath at every turn, or now in the fall, when the maples glow in red and golden glory. We here on the north side of Richmond are presented with a magnificence in the march of the seasons that inspires even the busiest among us just to stop and look and exclaim.

The question arises, therefore, as to how we should look at these wonders of seasonal beauty. Certainly we should enjoy them

---

This meditation was originally published in my book entitled *Preaching as Theology and Art* (Nashville: Abingdon Press, 1984). That book is now out of print, but I have retained the copyright.

and appreciate them and marvel at them, but even the atheists and pagans do that, and we have to ask if there is not a special way in which we as Christians should regard the world around us.

The question is not as simple as it may seem, for we Americans have always had a great deal of difficulty in coming to terms with the natural world. Most of the time as urban dwellers we simply ignore nature until God sets one of his trees on fire with color and demands that we take notice of it. Other times we idealize nature — our dime-store art testifies to that — and we refuse to recognize that the natural world is a realm of blood and fang and claw. In these times of ecology, we know that we have often considered the created world as simply an object to be manipulated by our technology. And worst of all, we have all, at some time or another, worshiped the natural world, supposedly finding God in its peace and beauty, mistakenly lifting up our eyes to the hills, as if somehow God were revealed in the eternal hills instead of in his Son Jesus Christ.

So it is not a simple question when we ask how we should regard the autumn splendors that appear outside this chapel, but perhaps our Scripture lesson for the morning can help us with the answer.

At the beginning and end of the flood story in Genesis, the Yahwist has provided us with two speeches of the Lord. The first of these speeches shows us the Creator of this world sobbing over his creation because every imagination of the thoughts of our heart is only evil continually.

You see, you and I do not know how to live in God's good creation. We scheme; we scheme how to get ahead in the world. With an attitude of what we consider to be great responsibility and wisdom, we carefully map out our day-to-day work and our own plans for the future. We calculate what we must do to secure a comfortable standard of living. We cultivate the friendship of those who are important and ignore the weak and unimportant. We make ourselves the center of the world and do everything to promote our own cause. And that, our Scripture lesson says, grieves God to his heart. He responds to our selfish attempts to run our own lives, apart from concern for him and our neighbor, not with wrath but with an aching heart and weeping over his children. As God weeps over Israel in the prophecies of Hosea and Jesus weeps over Jerusalem in the Gospel, so the Creator of this season of autumn weeps over us because we do not love him and our neighbor but love only our own sinful selves.

That means that God really should destroy us now, as he destroyed his creation in the days of Noah. He is sorry that he has made you and me. We really have not turned out as he wanted us to be. We have not at all lived up to his intentions for us. And so, according to our text, our end should be annihilation. God in his grief should do away with us and just start all over again.

But there is an amazing turn in the second part of our lesson from Genesis that changes everything for you and me. The human race does not improve after the salvation of Noah and his family from the flood. The imaginations of the thoughts of our heart are still evil from our youth. Even when we are pious students at Union Seminary, even when we serve the church, even when we think we do good, we are still self-centered children, running away from our Father and grieving him to his heart. But despite our continuing sin even after his redemption of us, we are told in this second text from Genesis that God does not wipe us out once and for all. Instead, he forgives and responds to our faithlessness simply with a promise: "I will never again destroy . . . every living creature as I have done. While the earth remains, seedtime and harvest, cold and heat, summer and winter, day and night, shall not cease" (Gen. 8:21-22).

That promise of forgiveness for all our sin was made real for us in Jesus Christ. There in the cross and resurrection, God manifested the mercy that now preserves us and our world, despite all our wrong against him. And the change of the seasons is an outward sign of God's redemption through his Son. Instead of punishing us for the weeping we constantly cause him, God turns the maples to red and gold. Instead of casting us out from his presence, he brings the birds south for the winter. Instead of sending us into darkness, he gives us a harvest moon and causes the stars to shine with special brightness in the crisp cold of autumn nights.

The season has moved into fall, and now the winter lies ahead, and after that the glory of spring and the heat of summer, because our God is merciful — because his response to our rebellion against him is not destruction of us and death but in Jesus Christ the loving preservation of everything he has made. "While the earth remains, seedtime and harvest, cold and heat, summer and winter, day and night, shall not cease." God sealed that promise with his Son.

And so how should we look at the world around us? Surely we should marvel and enjoy and exclaim. But above all we should praise our Creator, who in Jesus Christ has made this autumn and every season the manifestation of his marvelous mercy. Amen.

Sample Sermon

I preached this sermon on the Sunday of the Transfiguration in Harvard University's Memorial Church. It forms a bridge between the preceding chapter, which dealt with our sin, and the following chapter, which discusses the coming kingdom.

Between Despair and Illusion

Scripture Lessons:

2 Corinthians 4:1-18

Mark 9:2-9

I know a man who has a recurring nightmare. In that awful dream, he sees his grown children and their families hiding in a cave, huddling around a flickering fire. According to the dream, you see, the nuclear missiles have been fired. Civilization has been destroyed. And the man's children and grandchildren have been returned to the conditions of the Stone Age, only this time there will be no further evolution and no human progress, for the landscape that surrounds the man's heirs is totally dead from heat and radiation. The only outcome of anyone's survival will be wasting and inevitable death.

Well, what is your vision of the end of human history? Do you share that nuclear nightmare? Do you foresee a time when human folly has finally destroyed the earth — when, as Hollywood would have it, the world has become a planet of the apes? Or are you more realistic still? Do you believe that in the end the cockroaches will inherit the earth? Surely that is a vision which can leave us in despair, with no hope and therefore no meaning for our daily existence.

Or perhaps you have a more optimistic view of what is going to happen to the human race. Some persons think that eventually space-age creatures are going to come and rescue us — that they will bring with them a wisdom and a will to peace unknown to human beings, and that they will teach us how to get along with one another. You know — E.T., the savior of the world.

Others, of course, think that finally earth is going to be fair because our technology or education or science will have learned to overcome human fault. We will recombine our genes, some people think; or we will educate all to love one another; or we will develop a Star Wars system that will make nuclear destruction impossible. But of course the scientist goes home and quarrels with his wife at night, the teacher cannot control her classroom, and the Star Wars system turns into a flawed and unaffordable pipe dream. Human selfishness and pride and lust for power corrupt every lovely scheme. And we scan the heavens, looking and listening in vain for some saving signal from a distant galaxy.

Every ideal scheme for the future — the war to end all wars, the League of Nations, the UN, the classless society, the socialist or capitalist utopia — every dream of earth-made-good falls victim to human evil, and all our fantasies about a perfect world are shown finally to be illusions. Perhaps we have begun to realize how right Reinhold Niebuhr was when he told us that human sin would undermine every utopian revolution.

Between our despair and our illusions, however, there stands this story of the Transfiguration that we heard for our Scripture lesson from Mark. And surely it presents us with as strange a scene as any we have ever imagined. The setting of the story is heaven, and God's glory illumines every detaii. The high mount is the place of divine revelation. Jesus' robes shine glistening white, whiter than any earthly substance could bleach them. There is the voice of God speaking from the cloud to the three terrified disciples. But the time in the scene, its setting in the ages, is that time we have been discussing — the time of the end, when human history has been brought to its conclusion. In the symbolism of the story, the action takes place on the seventh day, that day when God has completed his work. And Jesus is seen talking to Moses and Elijah — that is, the sacred history of the law and the prophets has been fulfilled. In short, between our nightmares about the end and our illusory dreams for the future, God speaks a final word to us in this New Testament passage, and he tells us what the end of human history will really be like.

It will be that time, God says to us, when Jesus Christ reigns triumphant over the universe. "This is my beloved Son," God's voice says in our text. This is the Messiah, the King, the Lord. And so this is the One who will finally rule over heavens and earth and seas. Through him, God says, I made all persons and things; through him creation was accomplished. And so too, at the end, all creation will come to acknowledge that he is its Master. Jesus Christ, risen, victorious, Lord of all — that is the climax of this Epiphany season. That is the final vision of our history that God has given you and me to see.

Now we need to be very clear about what the passage does not tell us, of course. It does not tell us that we will avoid blowing up this planet. It makes no predictions about the route that economists and governments, military and terrorists will pursue. Indeed, the Bible is quite certain that sooner or later this earth will come to an end. "The heavens will vanish like smoke," wrote Isaiah; "the earth will wear out like a garment." But — the prophet continues with good news for humanity — "but my salvation will be for ever, and my deliverance will never be ended" (51:6). The world had its beginning from the Word of a God who is the Alpha and the Omega. He spoke his Word, and creation was accomplished, and at the end there will still be that Word, Jesus Christ, risen despite death's power and the whole force of evil that tried to kill him. Furthermore, our text assures us, there with Christ will be the disciples whom Jesus loves — Peter and James and John in our Gospel lesson — but now surely also the countless faithful, who in every age and every clime have called Jesus their Savior and trusted him to preserve their lives, though heaven and earth pass away. Yes, good Christians, yes, a sinful human race may blow this world off its axis. But at the end there will still be Christ our Lord, and with him eternal life for all those who love and trust him.

Our text from Mark also does not say that our technology and government, our science and education are futile, or that we should give up all our programs to improve human life on earth. After all, no other book in the world insists more on justice than does the Holy Bible. No other writing urges us more strongly to feed the hungry and clothe the naked and bring freedom to the oppressed. No other volume contains more visions of peace and wholeness for human beings. But what our Gospel lesson does tell us is that all our programs are provisional — that until Christ reigns, the kingdom of God will not have come on earth. And so we should not rest our ultimate hope on our sin-marred human schemes.

Every ideologue abroad in our society these days seems to believe that he or she has the final answer, just as every despot in history past has claimed that his or hers is the only way. But Jesus warned us against such human pretenders to his throne. "If any one says to you, 'Lo, here is the Christ!' or 'There he is!' do not believe it," Jesus taught. "For as the lightning comes from the east and shines as far as the west, so will be the coming of the Son of man" (Matt. 24:23, 27). In other words, we will know the transfigured Christ when he comes to establish his reign. And until he comes, no way is final and every human scheme and program for earth is provisional.

But Christ does come to rule. The Lord Jesus surely comes. And the message of this Transfiguration Sunday is that we can count with certainty on the fact that his will be the final victory. But we need to be very clear about just what that means, so we can have some hope on this blood-marked planet and therefore some reason for our living.

The fact that Christ will win the final victory means that waiting for us there at the end will be not some terrifying judge who checks off all the guilty offenses that you and I and this struggling world carry around with us daily. No, waiting for us there at the end will be the merciful Savior whom we have known so well from the Gospel stories — that One who would not condemn a woman caught in adultery, but who set her free to go and sin no more; that Master who washed a Judas's feet and who said "Peace" to the disciples who had denied and deserted him; that selfless love that forgave a thief from his cross and, yes, even his executioners. That One — that Jesus — will stretch out his pierced hands to us and welcome us sinners who trust him. Oh yes, when Jesus reigns, eternal mercy will rule the world.

And so too will the goodness of Christ become all in all. You know, our streets are so full of ugly evil. Society is bent out of shape with lies and deceit and broken promises. Children are abused, neglected, manipulated, turned into pornographic objects. The poor are made political pawns; the criminals write books and are celebrated. The tongues of the proud strut through the earth, and violence covers them like a garment. Over our earth hangs a blood-soaked pall. To be good is to be a joke. As Archie Bunker once said to his naive and innocent wife, "Edith, the world ain't ready for you yet." But you see, none of that is the last word. None of that will endure. For at the end of history is the Word of God, incarnated in our good Savior. All that we have known in Jesus — all that is lovely and pure, all that is just and honorable in Christ — will be the final shape of this earth. And every soul that trusts will sing the old hymn:

Beautiful Savior, Lord of the nations,
Son of God and Son of Man!
Glory and honor, praise, adoration,
Now and forevermore be thine!

The Transfiguration also tells us further that at the end there will be the power of Christ. Who can destroy him, dear friends? A Pilate tried. The Roman empire, Stalin, Hitler, Mao Tse-tung —

all attempted to erase his influence. And some walk among us today who would deny that he is their Lord. As Paul says in our Epistle lesson, the gospel is veiled only to those who are perishing, for the gods of this world have blinded their minds to keep them from seeing the light of the glory of Christ, who is the likeness of God. But Christ will not be buried, will he? This heedless world cannot get rid of him, and his is the power that will meet us there at the end — that power which healed the sick and raised the dead and opened the eyes that were blind; that power which changed a hate-filled Pharisee into Paul, the apostle to the world; that power which through the ages has transformed women and men and sent them out to teach and heal and preach; that power which has preserved his church, though the forces of hell within and without have tried to prevail against it. Meeting us at the end, good Christians, is the power of God in Jesus Christ, and so he will say to a new creation, "Be whole and good and just," and to our weak and weary spirits he will say, "Come and find rest for your souls." Yes, that is what the end of human history will really be like: Jesus Christ — merciful, good, powerful — and the kingdom of his love come on earth.

Now lest that all seem like just one more illusion or, perhaps better, too good to be true, let us also note how realistic is this Transfiguration story in our Gospel lesson. While the glory of God shines through its every line, at its beginning and end we find the dark shadows of suffering. During the week before the Transfiguration takes place, Jesus tells all his disciples that he must suffer many things and be rejected and crucified. And after Jesus and Peter and James and John come down from the mountain and go on their journey through Galilee toward Jerusalem, our Lord repeats the same realistic prediction: "The Son of Man will be delivered into the hands of men [and women], and they will kill him" (Mark 9:31). Golgotha, with its nails and its thirst, its blood and its mocking, still lies ahead, you see. After the Epiphany season, the church journeys toward Passion Week. We cannot remain on the mount of Transfiguration. We cannot just bask in the vision of the glory that is coming. Peter learned that on the mount when he tried to build those three dwelling places so they could remain there forever. No, the world is still very much with us, with all its awful corruption, and you and I still have to make our way through our tortured and, indeed, sometimes tempting landscape.

But we have had the vision, good Christians. We know what the end will be. God, by his Spirit, speaking through his Word, has shone in our hearts to give us the knowledge of the glory of God in the face of Jesus Christ. And so we know — we know that beyond the gore of Golgotha there is the glory of the resurrection. Beyond the murderous evil of this world there is the vital goodness of Jesus. Beyond the despair and illusions of human beings there is the coming rule of Christ.

Therefore, as Paul tells the Corinthian Christians, we need not lose heart. We may be afflicted in every way — and in this fallen world, we can always count on trials and afflictions — but we need never be crushed and we need never be hopeless. We need never think that broken lives or broken hearts or tears shed at some graveside are all there is to human life — the end, the finish, the final curtain. No, no, says Paul, for despite everything that he went through, he could write, "this slight momentary affliction is preparing for us an eternal weight of glory beyond all comparison" (2 Cor. 4:17).

We may be perplexed at times — unable to see God at work in any event of our history, unable to discern his hand in some sudden turn of our own daily road — but we need never be driven to despair. For behind it all, God is working steadily to fulfill his purpose, and he will bring us and our world to that good conclusion which he planned for us from the beginning.

We may even be persecuted for our faith, as Paul was persecuted and as countless Christians around the world today still share his martyrdom. We may be called to live the Christian way of life surrounded by a hostile society — I'm not sure that the Harvard campus always gladly welcomes a Christian presence in its midst — but we can be sure that we are never forsaken by our faithful God, who has called us to be his disciples and who will bring us at last to share life with our Lord in his eternal kingdom.

And so we are given that reassurance: "This is my beloved Son." But then there is that final command in our Gospel lesson: "Listen to him!" If we want to share in the hope and the final victory, then listen to Jesus Christ. Listen to his promises: "I will not leave you desolate; I will come to you. Where I am you will be also. I am the way, and the truth, and the life. Whoever lives and believes in me shall never die." Listen to the promises of Christ and know hope and peace in your souls — hope and assurance that the world can neither give nor ever take away.

And then listen, listen to the commands of Christ, and follow, follow daily. "Pray without ceasing. Love one another as I have loved you. Forgive seventy times seven. Teach all nations what I have commanded you. Take up your cross; lose your life for the gospel. Come. Follow me." For at the end, you see, at the end there will be still one more word and command: "Well done, thou good and faithful servant. Enter into the joy prepared for you."

Between our despair and our illusions about the goal of human history, God sets the glory of the transfigured Christ. He is God's beloved Son. Listen to him. Amen.

CHAPTER 7

The Final Question

We finally have to ask if God is truly Lord over his creation and if he does in fact have the power to restore it to the goodness that he intended for it in the beginning. Despite the marvelous grace, discussed at the end of the last chapter, with which the Creator continues to sustain his fallen universe, will our sinful corruption of our world finally overcome God's goodness, or will his loving purposes prevail to make his creation whole again? What is the world coming to? That is the final question.

The End of the Cosmos

Our scientists, most of whom are now convinced that the universe had a beginning, are also largely convinced that the expanding universe as we know it will have an end. They base this conclusion on the universal law of physics known as the second law of thermodynamics. According to this law, which is sometimes termed the law of entropy, all the energy differences which are the source of life, change, and activity in our universe will eventually be averaged out and disappear. For example, we light a log in the fireplace, which warms us as the wood's stored chemical energy is converted into heat. But eventually the fire goes out. The stored energy is exhausted. The heat is absorbed into the walls of the house and the surrounding atmosphere, and the whole system returns to a uniform temperature. The energy differences that we experienced as fire's cheery warmth are dissipated and cannot be recovered. So too with our universe. The process of the degradation of energy, as it is sometimes called, is going on throughout the universe continually, and eventually a state will be reached at which everything in the universe will be at the same temperature.[1] Thermodynamic equilibrium will have been reached, and there will be no possibility of producing the energy that nourishes the earth. The sun will have burned out, as will the stars, in this and every other galaxy, and there will be nothing left but cold, dark, expanding, near-empty space, populated at an ever-decreasing density by a few isolated chunks of ultra-dense matter and very little else.[2] As Paul Davies says, "It is a scenario that many scientists find profoundly depressing."[3]

Such a scenario will take place in four to five billion years if the cosmos continues to expand. But there is also an alternative that might be possible. It may be that the cosmos will not continue to expand, but that, having reached a static point, it will start to contract, slowly at first and then over many billions of years at an accelerated pace. Galaxies that are now moving away from one another will start to approach one another instead, constantly gathering speed. The resulting compression will elevate the temperature of the universe to a boiling point, and earth will become uninhabitable. As further shrinkage occurs, Davies explains, "the sky itself will begin to glow like a furnace, and the stars, embedded in this white hot space, will start to boil, then explode."[4] Finally, in a few hundred thousand years, the entire universe will shrivel into

1. George S. Hendry, *Theology of Nature* (Philadelphia: Westminster Press, 1980), p. 106.

2. Paul Davies, *God and the New Physics* (New York: Simon & Schuster, 1983), pp. 199-205.

3. Ibid., p. 204.

4. Ibid.

less than the space of an atom, whereupon space-time itself will disintegrate in what physicists call "the big crunch" — total annihilation and the end of the physical universe.[5]

In other words, the fate of the cosmos is to be either fried or frozen. But whatever the outcome, in such views, it also seems to be pointless. According to some, we should reconcile ourselves to such meaninglessness. Bertrand Russell expressed that resignation some years ago:

> All the labor of the ages, all the devotion, all the inspiration, all the noonday brightness of human genius is destined to extinction in the vast death of the solar system, and that the whole temple of Man's achievement must inevitably be buried beneath the debris of a universe in ruins — all these things, if not quite beyond dispute, are yet so nearly certain, that no philosophy which rejects them can hope to stand.[6]

Certainly if we reject such views, we can do so not on the basis of the scientific evidence but only on the basis of faith. And it is their own particular brand of faith that has led process theologians such as Philip Hefner[7] to postulate not science's cataclysmic end of the cosmos but a final universe of richness and complexity and perfection. Through the process of becoming, in which God is the urge toward newness, Hefner believes, God is perfecting and fulfilling the creation, constantly urging it toward the goal of his final consummation.[8] It is difficult to understand, however, how a God who is only contained in the processes of nature is able to transcend them and reverse their course.

It should be noted that we might find more optimism in the

5. Ibid., p. 205.

6. Russell, "A Free Man's Worship," in *Why I Am Not a Christian* (New York: Simon & Schuster, 1957), p. 107.

7. Hefner, "The Evolution of the Created Co-Creator," in *Cosmos as Creation: Theology and Science in Consonance*, ed. Ted Peters (Nashville: Abingdon Press, 1989), pp. 228-31.

8. Ibid., pp. 230-31.

notion of an oscillating universe. In such a view, the universe will bounce back out again to another cycle of expansion and reconstruction, and that process will go on *ad infinitum,* with ever new worlds coming into being and being destroyed.[9] But that theory also does nothing to give meaning to the universe in which we now live, because our particular universe will have about it no final goal or purpose.

When we turn to the biblical faith, we do find some seemingly contradictory texts concerning the continuing existence of our world. On the one hand, the Psalmists affirm that "the world is established; it shall never be moved" (93:1; cf. 78:69; 96:10; 104:5; 119:89-90). But as Psalms 93 and 104 show, those are expressions of trust in God's faithfulness and power to preserve the earth over against the forces of chaos that continually threaten it (cf. Ps. 65:6-7). The gaze of the Psalmists is fixed not so much on the final outcome (though Psalm 96 is concerned with that) as on present security in God's care.

Both Old Testament and New, on the other hand, do state that this world has an end, and in the texts that speak of the end of the world, its transitory nature is contrasted with the everlasting nature of God. Let me quote Psalm 102:25-27 (= Heb. 1:10-12) once again in this connection:

> Of old thou didst lay the foundation of the earth,
> and the heavens are the work of thy hands.
> They will perish, but thou dost endure;
> they will all wear out like a garment.
> Thou changest them like raiment, and they pass away;
> but thou art the same, and thy years have no end.

Similarly, Jesus affirmed that "heaven and earth will pass away, but my words will not pass away" (Mark 13:31 and parallels). Any theology, therefore, that binds the existence of God to the existence of the world — that sees God as the urge toward newness

9. Davies, *God and the New Physics,* p. 205.

in the evolutionary process, or that believes that God can be known only in, through, and under all things, or that identifies the divine with anything in all creation — falls before the biblical understanding of the eternity of God as contrasted with the transitory nature of the world.

Furthermore, no process or pantheistic or natural theology can offer the assurance that the biblical faith offers to our nuclear generation. We now have the power to turn the earth into a radioactive cinder. We may blow the earth off its axis, but God endures, says Second Isaiah, and he can take those who trust him into an everlasting fellowship:

> The heavens will vanish like smoke,
> the earth will wear out like a garment,
> and they who dwell in it will die like gnats;
> but my salvation will be for ever,
> and my deliverance will never be ended.
>
> (51:6)

This everlasting nature of God is the basis of surety in the Bible. Let us read Psalm 90 once again:

> Lord, thou hast been our dwelling place
> in all generations.
> Before the mountains were brought forth,
> or ever thou hadst formed the earth and the world,
> from everlasting to everlasting thou art God.
>
> (vv. 1-2)

Before there ever was a cosmos, there was God. And after the world we know is gone, there will still be God. On that foundation rest all of our hopes for eternity.

The main point is, however, that in their understandings of the existence of the cosmos, the Bible and modern science agree on two things: the world as we know it had a beginning, when time itself came into existence, and it will have an end.

The more apocalyptic passages of the Scriptures understand the end of the world in terms of God's final judgment on the sin of all:

> Behold, the Lord will lay waste the earth and make it desolate,
> and he will twist its surface and scatter its inhabitants. . . .
> The earth shall be utterly laid waste and utterly despoiled;
> for the Lord has spoken this word.
> The earth mourns and withers,
> the world languishes and withers;
> the heavens languish together with the earth.
> (Isa. 24:1, 3-4; cf. 10:23)

> The earth is utterly broken,
> the earth is rent asunder,
> the earth is violently shaken. . . .
> Its transgression lies heavy upon it,
> and it falls, and will not rise again.
> (Isa. 24:19-20)

In such Old Testament passages, despite the desolation wrought by God's judgment, there remains something of this world. But a passage such as 2 Peter 3:6-12, for example, while drawing on a Stoic tradition in which there is something like an oscillating universe, abandons that tradition to posit a complete end: "The heavens will pass away with a loud noise, and the elements will be dissolved with fire, and the earth and the works that are upon it will be burned up" (v. 10; cf. v. 7; Rev. 20:11).

Such final destruction of the cosmos might be compared to science's "big crunch," and while we comfort ourselves, as the Israelites did in Ezekiel's time, by saying, "He prophesies of times far off" (12:27), such a finale for the cosmos raises pressing questions for faith. Is God's judgment and final destruction of the cosmos the Lord's last word? Has his purpose to make a "very good" creation failed after all, and is God therefore unable to work his will, either for lack of power or for lack of love? To answer "yes" to any one of these questions would drastically change our understanding of the nature of God, for that would mean that God is ultimately unable to overcome the sin of the world and can do nothing other than destroy it. Our sin would have triumphed over the might and mercy of God, and everything that the Christian faith proclaims about redemption and eternal life would be called into question.

The Glad Good News

Certainly if God is bound up with this world and captive to it, science's scenario must be the final picture. A God enmeshed in the processes and things of nature will himself fall victim to nature's demise. But the Bible knows that God is not captive, and it also knows that God's judgment is not his final word. In short, it knows that the future goal of the world is not dependent on its present state — not even on the state of the world resulting from physics' laws or humans' sin. What nature is and what sinful human beings are will not determine the outcome of the cosmos. That is the glad good news from the Scriptures.

It seems to me that this is the profound view that the Scriptures express when they talk about God's creation of new heavens and a new earth (Isa. 65:17; 66:22; 2 Pet. 3:13; Rev. 21:1). Such statements are not so much a literalistic expression of the end of the cosmos and the creation of a totally new one as they are a confirmation of the fact that the God who transcends all creation is not bound by nature's processes or by what we would consider to be the inevitable results of human action and sin. God is not captive to past or present or inevitable future. Rather, he who created space-time in the beginning transcends his creation and will bring it to the resolution that he intended for it from the first. The new heavens and the new earth will not be the natural and inevitable outcome of this world, and certainly not the highest point in natural or human development. Rather, they will be the result of the breaking in of a new creative activity of God that will transform this world to accord with the divine purpose for it.

Moreover, our assurance of God's final and saving transformation of his world not only rests on his promise in the Scriptures of a new creation but also rests finally — as does the whole of Christian faith — on the resurrection of Jesus Christ. We see there in the story of the death and resurrection of our Lord the transmutation of all natural and historical inevitability. By our reckoning, human sin should have done Jesus forever to death. And by our natural science, the grave should have been the last word. But the power of God transcends all human and natural inevitability, and on the third day at dawn, Mary Magdalene and the other women find the tomb empty and their Lord risen to new life. Such is the resurrection's assurance that God can make all things new. Ted Peters has said it well:

> It is the experienced power of new life in the Easter resurrection that provides the foundation for our faith and trust in God to fulfill his promise to establish a new creation in the future. What does it take to raise the dead? What does it take to consummate history into a new and everlasting kingdom? It takes mastery over the created order. It takes a loving Father who cares but who is also a creator whose power is undisputed and unrivaled.[10]

If we use the resurrection as our paradigm for the future salvation of the cosmos — and in a sense, it is the only paradigm that we have — then it is also clear that God's new creation, while unbound from the past, also has some continuity with the past and the creation as we know it. The risen Christ shares something of the physical nature of this earth: the disciples see in his hands and side the marks of the nails and spear (John 20:20, 27), and he is present with Mary Magdalene and the disciples in a physical body, emphasized in Luke 24 and John 21 by his eating with his followers. And yet, the seeming body of this earth passes through

10. Peters, "Cosmos as Creation," in *Cosmos as Creation*, p. 72.

locked doors (John 20:19) and can suddenly appear and disappear. In the new creation there is some continuity with the old creation, and yet there is also a physicality that is radically new and different. Paul is saying the same thing when he talks in 1 Corinthians 15 of the transformation of the physical, terrestrial, perishable body into the spiritual, celestial, imperishable body in the resurrection of the faithful. The new creation has some continuity with the creation as we now know it, and yet it will be radically different.

It is not, therefore, the case that when the biblical writers speak of God's creation of new heavens and a new earth, they are confessing God's inability to fulfill his purposes for this sinful and fallen world. That is taking the apocalypticism of the Scriptures too far. Rather, the biblical writers are using the apocalyptic language of their day — indeed, straining at the limits of that language — to express the qualitatively new that God will introduce into the old, unfettered by the sinful inevitability and natural processes of the old. All powers in nature and history are subject to the God who made and sustains them, and the Bible's good news is that he will transform them and make them all new.

As a result, we find in the Scriptures a constant tension between the thought that God's final salvation will consist in the *transformation* of this world and the belief that salvation will consist in the total *replacement* of this world. In the Isaianic collection of traditions, for example, all three Isaianic writers speak of nature and history transformed (2:2-4; chap. 35; 40:4; 41:17-20, et al.; 60:1-7, 19-20; 65:17-25), and yet, that transformation is also pictured in terms of new heavens and a new earth. Perhaps the tension is best encapsulated in some closing verses of Third Isaiah:

> For as the new heavens and the new earth
>   which I will make
> shall remain before me, says the Lord;
>   so shall your descendants and your name remain.
> From new moon to new moon,
>   and from sabbath to sabbath,

> all flesh shall come to worship before me,
> says the Lord.
>
> (66:22-23)

We see in these verses that historical Israel, with its worship, and all nations are present — the old world has not totally disappeared. And yet, there is a radical newness, a virtual new creation.

So too, in the New Testament, the final picture is of a new heaven and a new earth, for the first heaven and the first earth have passed away (Rev. 21:1). As a result, the faithful can be called strangers and exiles on the face of the present earth, "aliens and exiles" (1 Pet. 2:11; cf. 1:17), whose final home is not the sphere of this world (John 18:36; cf. 3:3) but that "city which has foundations, whose builder and maker is God" (Heb. 11:10). Yet, Jesus' prayer is that "Thy kingdom come, Thy will be done, on *earth* as it is in heaven" (Matt. 6:10, my emphasis), and it is this *earth* that the meek shall inherit (Matt. 5:5), not some ethereal realm.

In short, just as the Scriptures never understand salvation in terms of some ascetic escape from the life of the world or in terms of some mystical absorption into Nirvana or the divine Om, so too they never totally abandon this world as hopeless, despite their apocalyptic borrowings. The life of this earth has not been a meaningless mistake, which God will then desert in his creation of new life in a new world and universe. To be sure, there are places in the Scriptures where God is tempted to abandon his creation and just make a new one — for example, in the story of the flood in Genesis, or in his dealings with rebellious Israel in the wilderness (Num. 14:12). Yet, the divine Mercy persists and will not give up on his universe or his people in it. And the goal toward which God steadily works is the salvation of all that he has made, its freeing from the bondage of decay and death to which our sin has subjected it (Rom. 8:21-23), and its transformation into the good and abundant wholeness that God intended for it in the beginning. God brings in a kingdom that is not of this world and yet that will transform this world to accord with his purpose for it.

That of which the Scriptures are certain, moreover, is that human beings cannot create the new world. Richard Cartwright Austin has written that it is finally a moral "ecology of integrity," inspired by the example of Christ, that "will prevail over the depredations of the powerful who strip-mine the biosphere," and that "integrity will redeem the course of history — as naked power cannot — and will achieve a just society."[11] Others place their hope in the ability of science so to manipulate human DNA that we produce human beings who know how to live in harmony with the natural world and with each other.

Even more utopian are the views of certain radical feminist historians who have rewritten history in the belief that it will furnish them with the motive power to create a new world in the present. There was, they believe, anywhere between 30,000 and 200,000 years ago (their figures vary widely), a golden age of "goddess culture" in which society was matriarchal, peaceful, and egalitarian under the rule of the great Goddess. All were one with nature and with one another. Harmony ruled. Both nature and human beings participated in the divine. Persons followed peaceful agricultural pursuits. Peace covered the earth — until it all was disrupted by the male-dominated political state, in which occupational specialization, commerce, social stratification, and militarism developed. In short, patriarchy disrupted the natural order; patriarchy ruined the earth. But empowered by this vision of the supposed golden past, such feminists believe they can re-create it[12] and "return to human possibilities lost at the dawn of history" (Rosemary Ruether).[13] The rediscovery of this past "signals a way out of our alienation from one another and from nature," agrees Riane Eisler.[14]

11. Austin, *Hope for the Land: Nature in the Bible,* Environmental Theology Series, Book 3 (Atlanta: John Knox Press, 1988), p. 231.

12. Elizabeth Kristol, "History in the Past Perfect," *First Things,* no. 12, April 1991, pp. 47-49. Kristol refutes such ideas.

13. Ruether, cited by Kristol in ibid., p. 49.

14. Eisler, cited by Kristol in ibid.

Very similar and equally utopian are the views of those deep ecologists who view the earth as having been ruined not by males solely but by Man; human beings with their civilization have exploited and destroyed the natural world. Thus, the slogan of the group called Earth First is "Back to the Pleistocene," back to the time when human beings were simply hunters and gatherers.[15] Indeed, ecotopian Paul Shepherd has worked out a detailed plan "to remodel life after early hunter-gatherer societies, urging that the entire world's population (which he would like to see stabilized at eight billion people) cluster along the coastlines of the continents, leaving the interiors untouched by human habitations."[16] Then the earth would become "good" again, believe the deep ecologists, and the life of human beings and nature would be as it was meant to be.

Such views sound very silly, but their basic presupposition about human beings is not totally unique, because most of the special-interest groups of our time believe that their particular program or ideology is the key to creating utopia on earth. If we can just get rid of sexism or racism, militarism or capitalism, colonialism or nationalism, communism or socialism, or any other of the isms and problems — hunger, poverty, illiteracy, disease — to which human beings fall victim, then they believe we can construct the ideal society, at harmony within itself and with the world of nations and nature around it. But every human utopia falls victim to human sin, and every ideal, selfless dream is marred by the reality of human selfishness. As Genesis 3:24 so profoundly portrays it, there are now guards at the re-entrance into paradise, and nothing human beings can do can get rid of the guards. Only God, who put the guards there, can remove them. Many would claim that they are such gods or goddesses, at one with the divine that lives and moves in all things. But it was that claim to divinity which made the guards to the garden necessary in the first place (Gen. 3:5, 22), and the proud

15. Ibid., p. 46.
16. Ibid., p. 47.

and sinful claim on the part of us creatures to be our own deities only compounds the problem. In the words of Jesus, "Those who want to save their life will lose it, and those who lose their life for my sake, and for the sake of the gospel, will save it" (Mark 8:35, NRSV, and parallels). The new world, the kingdom of God for which we pray, will come on earth even as it is in heaven only as the result of the action of God. Only the One who is not captive to the world can save the world.

It is this biblical affirmation that prevents all human self-righteousness. We are constantly bidden throughout the Scriptures to work for the healing of nature and of human society, and we are assured that our labors for the Lord are never in vain (1 Cor. 15:58; Phil. 4:8-9; 2 Chron. 15:7). But because the kingdom has not yet come and because God alone can bring it, we also know that all human programs, institutions, and constructions are provisional and imperfect, either to be judged and replaced or to be gathered up and perfected in God's final transformation and reconstruction of his world.

At the same time, it is this biblical affirmation of God's final work that prevents all despair, for the kingdom is coming and will surely come. It has begun to come in the person of Jesus Christ (Mark 1:15; Luke 11:20; 17:21; John 18:36), and in his resurrection he has defeated all the powers of evil and disorder, of decay and death that would defeat God's final rule. He is the new Adam, through whom God forgives and transforms the human race. By the first Adam, sin and death entered the world; by the second Adam shall all things and persons be made alive and new (1 Cor. 15:22, 45; 2 Cor. 5:17). All authority in heaven and on earth has been given to him (Matt. 28:18; Luke 10:22; John 3:35; 13:3; Rom. 14:9; Phil. 2:9-10), and as in the beginning all things were created through him, so at the end all things will be re-created through him:

> For as in Adam all die, so also in Christ shall all be made alive. But each in his own order: Christ the first fruits, then at his coming those who belong to Christ. Then comes the end, when

> he delivers the kingdom to God the Father after destroying every rule and every authority and power. For he must reign until he has put all his enemies under his feet. The last enemy to be destroyed is death. "For God has put all things in subjection under his feet." (1 Cor. 15:22-27)

Once again we should note, in this quotation from Paul, that the new age will have a continuity with the world which has gone before, represented in the figure and type of Adam, and yet that which comes at the end will be radically new. But the end, the final kingdom, surely comes, and because of that joyful prospect, Christians are delivered from that despair over the meaninglessness and futility of the world which threatens to defeat the rest of humanity (cf. 2 Cor. 4:7-12; 5:1-5).

By using the figure of the new Adam, Paul connects Christ with this world, but he also emphasizes Christ's transcendence in 1 Corinthians 15:47 ("The first man was from the earth, a man of dust; the second man is from heaven"), and that once again accords with the Bible's consistent affirmation that only God can bring in the new age.

Such transcendence is also emphasized by the cosmic disturbances that always accompany God's theophany in the Bible and that will accompany the second coming of our Lord to establish his kingdom on earth. As I briefly mentioned in Chapter 5, according to the Old Testament, when God appears, the whole cosmos acknowledges his lordly presence. Thus this is the description of the descent of the Lord to Sinai to enter into covenant with his people:

> And Mount Sinai was wrapped in smoke, because the Lord descended upon it in fire; and the smoke of it went up like the smoke of a kiln, and the whole mountain quaked greatly. And as the sound of the trumpet grew louder and louder, Moses spoke, and God answered him in thunder. (Exod. 19:18-19)

Or there is this from a prophetic theophanic vision recorded in Psalm 97:

Clouds and thick darkness are round about him;
righteousness and justice are the foundation of his throne.
Fire goes before him,
and burns up his adversaries round about.
His lightnings lighten the world;
the earth sees and trembles.
The mountains melt like wax before the Lord,
before the Lord of all the earth.

(vv. 2-5)

Indeed, in Habakkuk 3, which is the prophet's vision of the coming of the final rule of God, all nature and nations give way before his power:

He stood and measured the earth;
he looked and shook the nations;
then the eternal mountains were scattered,
the everlasting hills sank low. . . .
Thou didst cleave the earth with rivers.
The mountains saw thee, and writhed. . . .
The sun and moon stood still in their habitation. . . .
Thou didst trample the sea with thy horses,
the surging of mighty waters.

(vv. 6, 9, 10, 11, 15)

This is no God contained in the processes of nature or identified with his creation. This is the Creator God before whose lordship all nature and nations bow. (Cf. Judg. 5:4-5; 2 Sam. 22:8-16 = Ps. 18:7-15; Ps. 68:7-8; 77:16-19; Ezek. 38:19-20.)

So it is too in the New Testament when Christ, through whom all things were made, returns to rule his creation. When he comes again to set up his kingdom, his appearance will be preceded by the disruption of nature's ways:

The sun will be darkened, and the moon will not give its light, and the stars will be falling from heaven, and the powers in the heavens

> will be shaken. And then they will see the Son of man coming in clouds with great power and glory. And then he will send out the angels, and gather his elect from the four winds, from the ends of the earth to the ends of heaven. (Mark 13:24-27 and parallels)

The new age that comes will be a radical interruption of the processes and powers of this world, and the inbreaking of a new reality which only God can create.

The Character of the New Age

The pictures that the Scriptures draw of the character of God's coming kingdom are not imaginative projections of human wishes and desire but are finally all based on the church's experience with the person of Jesus Christ. In him, the church has experienced proleptically the first fruits of that which will finally come. In him, the church has learned what the world is coming to. (See the preceding sermon on Christ's transfiguration.) To Christians in Christ has been revealed what the final outcome of nature and history will be:

> "What no eye has seen, nor ear heard,
> nor the heart of man conceived,
> what God has prepared for those who love him,"
> God has revealed to us through the Spirit.
> (1 Cor. 2:9-10)

> For he has made known to us in all wisdom and insight the mystery of his will, according to his purpose which he set forth in Christ as a plan for the fulness of time, to unite all things in him, things in heaven and things on earth. (Eph. 1:9-10)

As a means of organizing the Scriptures' views of the new age, we could use one of their leading motifs and describe God's coming kingdom in terms of the conquest of chaos — of God's final triumph over those forces of evil, darkness, disorder, and death under which our present world still suffers.

Both Old Testament and New are very sure that at the end, God will do away with the chaos — the non-life, the dark void of nothingness — which he first put in check by his power at the initial creation and yet which continues to threaten our fallen world. For example, we read in Isaiah 27 that the chaos, pictured in terms of the serpent or Leviathan of the chaos dragon myth, will be finally slain:

> In that day the Lord with his hard and great and strong sword will punish Leviathan the fleeing serpent, Leviathan the twisting serpent, and he will slay the dragon that is in the sea. (v. 1)

That is a future hope in the book of Isaiah, but when the Christ comes, he therefore stills the chaotic waters (Mark 4:35-41), his light shines in the darkness of chaos and the darkness cannot overcome him (John 1:5), and at the end, therefore, in the new heavens and the new earth, the sea — the chaos — will be no more (Rev. 21:1).

1. Evil Gone

God will do away with the sin and *evil* of chaos that have so infected our world (Isa. 11:4). In the Old Testament, God's final judgment on and destruction of the wicked is pictured most often in terms of the coming of the Day of the Lord. Isaiah 2:6-22 and Zephaniah 1:14-18 are probably the classic portrayals of the Day's judgment, but there is also this from Malachi:

> For behold, the day comes, burning like an oven, when all the arrogant and all evildoers will be stubble; the day that comes shall burn them up, says the Lord of hosts, so that it will leave them neither root nor branch. (4:1)

Among those things that are to be destroyed are all the idols to whom men and women have given their hearts, rather than to God:

> And on that day, says the Lord of hosts, I will cut off the names of the idols from the land, so that they shall be remembered no more. (Zech. 13:2; cf. Isa. 17:8; 30:22)

"For I will remove the names of the Baals from her [Israel's] mouth, and they shall be mentioned by name no more" (Hos. 2:17) — a significant promise for all those in our day who would identify God with the life of nature.

According to Ezekiel, however, we all need cleansing from our idolatry and sinful ways, and this is a cleansing that God will effect by giving us a new heart and spirit:

> From all your idols I will cleanse you. A new heart I will give you, and a new spirit I will put within you; and I will remove from your body the heart of stone and give you a heart of flesh. I will put my spirit within you, and make you follow my statutes and be careful to observe my ordinances. . . . And you shall be my people, and I will be your God. (36:25-28, NRSV)

Indeed, the Bible sees no hope of anyone enduring God's final judgment apart from God's merciful and thoroughgoing transformation of them: "Who can endure the day of his coming, and who can stand when he appears? For he is like a refiner's fire and like fullers' soap; he will sit as a refiner and purifier of silver" (Mal. 3:2-3). In Jeremiah's new covenant, therefore, it is necessary that God forgive us and write his law upon our hearts, so that we all can know him and walk according to his commandments (31:31-34).

Surely this is the necessity for Christians also when confronted with the New Testament's similar announcement of the coming judgment in the Day of the Lord. For the New Testament too is quite convinced that all face a final reckoning before God:

> We will all stand before the judgment seat of God. For it is written,
>
> "As I live, says the Lord, every knee shall bow to me,

> and every tongue shall give praise to God."
> So then, each of us will be accountable to God.
> (Rom. 14:10-12, NRSV; cf. 2:5; Isa. 45:23; Phil. 2:10-11; 1 Cor. 3:13)

That reckoning will be carried out in Christ Jesus when he comes again "to judge the living and the dead":

> While God has overlooked the times of human ignorance, now he commands all people everywhere to repent, because he has fixed a day on which he will have the world judged in righteousness by a man whom he has appointed, and of this he has given assurance to all by raising him from the dead. (Acts 17:30-31, NRSV)

> For all of us must appear before the judgment seat of Christ, so that each may receive recompense for what has been done in the body, whether good or evil. (2 Cor. 5:10, NRSV; cf. 1 Cor. 4:5; Rom. 2:16; 2 Tim. 4:1)

> The hour is coming when all who are in the tombs will hear his voice and come forth, those who have done good, to the resurrection of life, and those who have done evil, to the resurrection of judgment. (John 5:28-29)

So it is that many of Jesus' parables pose the question of whether we will live or die eternally in terms of whether or not we receive him in faith (e.g., Matt. 13:36-43; Mark 4:1-20; Luke 18:1-8), and the great assize of Matthew 25:31-46, which is often misinterpreted individualistically, portrays the judgment of *all nations* in terms of the decision about and action toward the *disciples* of Jesus ("my brethren"), because "as you did it to one of the least of these my brethren, you did it to me" (v. 40). Those who have refused the gospel and its servants will be told, "Depart from me, you cursed, into the eternal fire prepared for the devil and his angels" (v. 41). Indeed, the Gospel according to John sees the decision of belief or unbelief about Jesus as the Christ, the Son of God, as determinative already in the present of our final fate (20:31):

> Now is the judgment of this world, now shall the ruler of this world be cast out. . . . He who rejects me and does not receive my sayings has a judge; the word that I have spoken will be his judge on the last day. (12:31, 48)

God will do away with the wicked and evil when Christ comes to establish his kingdom, and the decision about Jesus Christ and faithfulness or unfaithfulness toward his gospel will be the measure by which the judgment is carried out:

> Those who are ashamed of me and of my words in this adulterous and sinful generation, of them the Son of Man will also be ashamed when he comes in the glory of his Father with the holy angels. (Mark 8:38, NRSV; cf. Matt. 10:33; Luke 12:9)

Consonant with the thought of the Old Testament, we have hope of standing in the face of such judgment only by God's forgiveness of us by the cross and resurrection of Jesus Christ — which is the fulfillment of Jeremiah's new covenant — and by God's thoroughgoing transformation of our lives through the gift of his Spirit. God has "given us his Spirit in our hearts as a guarantee," exults Paul (2 Cor. 1:22), and has written the Spirit not on tablets of stone but on our human hearts (2 Cor. 3:3; cf. Jer. 31:33), so that we now have that knowledge of God promised by Jeremiah (2 Cor. 4:6) and can call God "Father" (Gal. 4:6) and walk obediently in his ways (Gal. 5:22-24). God alone by his work can keep our hearts and minds in Christ Jesus (Phil. 4:7) and establish our "hearts unblamable in holiness before our God and Father, at the coming of our Lord Jesus with all his saints" (1 Thess. 3:13).

Because Paul knows that Christ dwells in him by the Spirit (Gal. 2:20), it is therefore written of him in 2 Timothy that there is laid up for him the crown of righteousness, which the Lord, the righteous Judge, will award to him on that Day, and not only to him but also to all who have loved the Lord (4:8). Only in that faith is there salvation from the final judgment of Christ when he comes to destroy the evil of chaos from the earth and to set up his kingdom.

2. *Darkness Ended*

There is also the persistent note throughout the Scriptures that God's salvation of his world will mean the end of the *darkness* of chaos, that darkness which was upon the face of the great *tehom* or chaotic waters in the beginning (Gen. 1:2) and which symbolized all lifelessness and evil opposed to God's light and life and good.

God and his Word are the source of light, according to the Bible (Gen. 1:3; Mic. 7:8; Mal. 4:2; Luke 1:79; John 1:4, 7, 9, et passim; 2 Cor. 4:6; Eph. 5:8, 14; 1 Pet. 2:9). Indeed, God is the "Father of lights" (James 1:17) "who . . . dwells in unapproachable light" (1 Tim. 6:16) and with whom there is no shadow of turning. And so the constant call of the Scriptures is, "Come, let us walk in the light of the Lord" (Isa. 2:5), for "every one who does evil hates the light. . . . But he who does what is true comes to the light" (John 3:20-21).

But the figure of God as the source of light has nothing to do with the sun and moon and stars in the Bible's thought (compare Gen. 1:3 with vv. 14-19). Rather, God's light is associated with his glory, the shining effulgence of his presence (Isa. 60:2), and it is given also by his Word (Gen. 1:3), and both of these thoughts are encompassed in the presentation of the incarnate Word as the "light" in whom we have beheld his glory "as of the only Son from the Father" (John 1:4, 14). This light from God and his Word therefore is given only to the faithful who receive the Word (Exod. 10:23; Jer. 13:16; Job 29:1-4), while it is withheld from the wicked who reject the Word (Lam. 3:1-6).

The thought of the Bible, therefore, is that in God's kingdom, the light of the sun and moon and stars will no longer be necessary:

> The sun shall be no more
> your light by day,
> nor for brightness shall the moon
> give light to you by night,
> but the Lord will be your everlasting light,
> and your God will be your glory.
>
> (Isa. 60:19; cf. Zech. 14:7)

> And the city has no need of sun or moon to shine upon it, for the glory of God is its light, and its lamp is the Lamb [i.e., the Word]. By its light shall the nations walk; and the kings of the earth shall bring their glory into it, and its gates shall never be shut by day — and there shall be no night there. (Rev. 21:23-25)

In the kingdom of God there will be no night. The darkness of chaos will be gone forever. Perhaps no more radical statement of the newness and transcendence of God's new creation could be formulated.

3. *Disorder Done*

God's new age will also be marked by peace and security and wholeness, and chaos's *disorder* and disruption of the world will be things of the past. As a result, the corruption of all of God's good gifts, pictured for us in the primeval history of Genesis 3–11, will be healed. The primeval history portrayed the dissolution of all human community — between husband and wife (Gen. 3), between brother and brother, among all societies (Gen. 4), and among all nations (Gen. 11). But the dream of the Old Testament prophets is that all nations will come together in one human community of justice and righteousness under God's direction (Isa. 2:2-4 = Mic. 4:1-3; cf. Isa. 19:23-24; 44:1-5; Zech. 8:20-23). Therefore war will be abolished forever (Hos. 2:18; Isa. 9:5; cf. Ps. 46:8-10), and "they shall all sit under their own vines and under their own fig trees, and no one shall make them afraid" (Mic. 4:4, NRSV).

> Then justice will dwell in the wilderness,
> and righteousness abide in the fruitful field.
> And the effect of righteousness will be peace,
> and the result of righteousness, quietness and trust for ever.
> (Isa. 32:16-17)

God is a God of peace, according to the Bible (Isa. 9:6; Rom. 15:33; 2 Cor. 13:11; Phil. 4:9; 1 Thess. 5:23; cf. 2 Thess. 3:16), and the gospel is a gospel of peace (Eph. 6:15). So when the Savior of the world is born in Bethlehem, he comes to bring the peace of God (Luke 2:14; cf. John 14:27) and to "guide our feet into the way of peace" (Luke 1:79). Not only does he give us peace with God through his cross and resurrection (Rom. 5:1; Col. 1:20), healing sin's alienation of us from our Maker, but he also heals sin's alienation of wife from husband (Gal. 3:28), of sibling from sibling (Matt. 5:21-24), of community member from community member (Eph. 6:23; Heb. 12:14; 1 John), and of race from race (Eph. 2:14-15). The fruit of his Spirit is peace, love, kindness, goodness, and self-control (Gal. 5:22-23). His kingdom will be characterized by righteousness and peace and joy in the Holy Spirit (Rom. 14:17).

Ian Barbour has written that "death and suffering are necessary conditions of life in an evolutionary world,"[17] and if one is a process theologian as Barbour is, then death and suffering will always be expected to be present in nature's ways. But the radical newness of the kingdom envisioned by the Scriptures forms an entirely different picture in which suffering is a thing of the past:

> "Behold, the dwelling of God is with men [and women]. He will dwell with them, and they shall be his people, and God himself will be with them; he will wipe away every tear from their eyes, and death shall be no more, neither shall there be mourning nor crying nor pain any more, for the former things have passed away." (Rev. 21:3-4; cf. Isa. 35:10)

This means that nature, which was corrupted and fell with our human fall, will be healed and all physical life will be restored to its original goodness. No longer will there be those physical and genetic maladies that lead to illness and suffering; but the deaf will hear, the blind see, the lame walk, and the dumb speak (Isa. 29:18; 32:3; 35:5-6), a healing begun in the ministry of Jesus

17. Barbour, *Religion in an Age of Science,* the Gifford Lectures, vol. 1 (San Francisco: Harper & Row, 1990), p. 204.

(Matt. 11:5; 15:31; Mark 2:1-12; John 5:8-9; 9:1-7; et al.). Indeed, even the "mind of the rash will have good judgment," says Isaiah, "and the tongue of the stammerers will speak readily and distinctly. The fool will no more be called noble, nor the knave said to be honorable" (32:4-5): both bodies and minds will be made whole. God will bind up the hurt and wounds of his people (30:26), sickness will be done away (33:24), and none will suffer calamity or premature death (65:20; cf. v. 23; Jer. 31:16).

There will be no hunger in the kingdom of God (Ezek. 34:29; cf. Isa. 49:10), for the transformed earth will blossom forth in a paradisaical fruitfulness (Isa. 32:15; 41:17-20; et al.) given it by the Lord of all nature:

> And I will provide for them prosperous plantations so that they shall no more be consumed with hunger in the land, and no longer suffer the reproach of the nations. (Ezek. 34:29)

> They shall come and sing aloud on the height of Zion,
> and they shall be radiant over the goodness of the Lord,
> over the grain, the wine, and the oil,
> and over the young of the flock and the herd;
> their life shall be like a watered garden,
> and they shall languish no more.
> Then shall the maidens rejoice in the dance,
> and the young men and the old shall be merry.
> I will turn their mourning into joy,
> I will comfort them, and give them gladness for sorrow.
> I will feast the soul of the priests with abundance,
> and my people shall be satisfied with my goodness, says the Lord.
>
> (Jer. 31:12-14)

In other words, no longer will nature fight against human beings in the kingdom of God, but by the action of its Maker and Sustainer, it will yield its abundance. Indeed, the picture of the kingdom in the New Testament is often that of a feast (Matt. 8:11

and parallel; 25:1-13 — cf. Luke 12:35-38; Matt. 22:1-14 and parallel; Mark 14:25 and parallels; Rev. 19:9), a picture of joy and satisfaction of physical want well captured in Isaiah:

> On this mountain the Lord of hosts will make for all peoples a feast of fat things, a feast of wine on the lees, of fat things full of marrow, of wine on the lees well refined. (25:6)

We sometimes wonder that the One who inaugurated the kingdom of God on earth was called "a glutton and a drunkard" (Matt. 11:19 and parallel), but surely in him was manifested the abundant life of the kingdom — those waters for the thirsty, that wine and milk that can be had without price, and the bread that satisfies from the hand of God (Isa. 55:1-2).

Not only will the antagonism between human beings and the soil, which was first noted in Genesis 3 and 4, be healed in the kingdom of God, but in God's new world, humankind will once again be set at peace with the animal kingdom, in contrast to Genesis 9:2. Varying pictures in the Old Testament set forth this thought. On the one hand, wild beasts will be prohibited from endangering the life of the people of God. "No lion shall be there, nor shall any ravenous beast," promises Isaiah 35:9. And there is this from Ezekiel:

> I will make with them [Israel] a covenant of peace and banish wild beasts from the land, so that they may dwell securely in the wilderness and sleep in the woods. . . . They shall no more be a prey to the nations, nor shall the beasts of the land devour them; they shall dwell securely, and none shall make them afraid. (34:25, 28)

Such statements imply that other creatures are still a threat to humankind.

On the other hand, Hosea pictures the final redemption as a time when God has stilled the conflict between human beings and other creatures on the earth:

> And I will make for you a covenant on that day with the beasts of the field, the birds of the air, and the creeping things of the ground. (2:18)

That is certainly the thought also of Isaiah:

> The wolf shall dwell with the lamb,
> and the leopard shall lie down with the kid,
> and the calf and the lion and the fatling together,
> and a little child shall lead them.
> The cow and the bear shall feed;
> their young shall lie down together;
> and the lion shall eat straw like the ox.
> (11:6-7)

Interestingly enough, Wisdom theology, represented by the speech of Eliphaz in Job 5, understands this peace with the animal world to be available already to all of those who walk by Wisdom and thus avoid sin against God:

> [You] shall not fear the wild animals of the earth.
> For you shall be in league with the stones of the field,
> and the wild animals shall be at peace with you.
> You shall know that your tent is safe,
> you shall inspect your fold and miss nothing.
> (vv. 23-24, NRSV)

In most passages, however, the thought is connected only with God's coming kingdom, in which God has created not only peace among human beings and the animal world but also peace among the wild beasts themselves, so that lion and calf can lie down together, with the calf fearing no harm from the lion. Wisdom's thought that peace with the animal world is the result of the absence of human sin is exactly in line with the whole Scripture's understanding, however, as we have previously noted. Nature fell when human beings fell; our rebellion against God ruined the world. And so in the kingdom of God, when sin will be done away, the kingdom of nature will be peaceable. This is what Isaiah means when he says that "the sucking child shall play over the hole of the asp,/and the weaned child shall put his hand on the adder's den" (11:8) — the serpent of our sin, recalling Genesis 3, will be turned into harmlessness; the sin of humankind will be no more.[18] Thus Isaiah can add his glad promise:

> They shall not hurt or destroy
> in all my holy mountain;
> for the earth shall be full of the knowledge of the Lord
> as the waters cover the sea.
>
> (11:9; cf. 65:25)

Because nature will share in the final salvation of humankind in the kingdom, the Old Testament repeatedly portrays the natural world as rejoicing at God's final transformation of his world. This is very characteristic of the Isaiah traditions, in which desert and mountains rejoice in gladness at the final coming of their Creator King (35:1-2) and his salvation of his people (55:12-13):

> Sing for joy, O heavens, and exult, O earth;
> break forth, O mountains, into singing!
> For the Lord has comforted his people,
> and will have compassion on his afflicted.
>
> (49:13)

But it is also very characteristic of those psalm hymns that look forward to the Lord's final coming:

> Let the heavens be glad, and let the earth rejoice;
> let the sea roar, and all that fills it;

18. When the Isaianic tradition of Isaiah 65:25 quotes from Isaiah 11:6-9, the serpent figure is altered to refer to an actual serpent that will continue to eat the dust of judgment, as in Genesis 3:14. But this is apparently an isolated text, inconsistent with other pictures of the final salvation.

> let the field exult, and everything in it!
> Then shall all the trees of the wood sing for joy
> before the Lord, for he comes,
> for he comes to judge the earth.
> He will judge the world with righteousness,
> and the peoples with his truth.
> (96:11-13; cf. 98:7-9)

The natural world and all its creatures will shout praise to the Lord who made them and who will come to release them from their "groaning in travail" and their "bondage to decay" and death (Rom. 8:20-23).

4. Death Defeated

When we ask what the world is coming to, we can affirm from the Scriptures that it is finally coming into joy. And we could sum up all that has gone before by saying that at the end of our history, when God comes in Jesus Christ to set up his kingdom in a transformed world, *death,* that last, final vestige of chaos, will be gone forever. "The last enemy to be destroyed is death," writes Paul (1 Cor. 15:26), and so in Revelation's vision of the end, the Son of Man proclaims,

> "Fear not, I am the first and the last, and the living one; I died, and behold I am alive for evermore, and I have the keys of Death and Hades." (1:17-18)

Death and Hades will be thrown into the lake of fire — their final destruction (cf. Heb. 2:14), called a "second death" (Rev. 20:14). And in the new heavens and new earth, death will be no more (Rev. 21:4; cf. 2 Tim. 1:10).

Death, if we think of it in terms of the void and nothingness and non-being of the biblical chaos, is finally what would render this universe of ours meaningless, as I said at the beginning of this chapter: that this world so teeming with billions of forms of life, so fecund in its order, so marked with beauty and design, so full of powerful forces, should finally end either fried or frozen — that would mean that there has been no point to it all. And that human life, with all its work and cares, its loves and hatreds and dreams, its dear relationships and sacrifices, its sufferings and joys and struggles, should finally have no meaning and disappear into nothingness — that is the terrible threat which death poses for all God's creation. Death gained its power finally to do away with all life when humankind turned away from God — turned away from the one Source of life and wandered into a world where human mortality tried to become sovereign. And the whole cosmos felt the shackles of eternal death fastened to it. But as sin came into the world through the human race and with it eternal death, the wages of sin (Rom. 5:12; 6:21), so life was restored to the world by God made man in Jesus Christ, who conquered sin and death. The goal and purpose of the entire cosmos, with all its creatures, depend on one event — namely, Christ's resurrection:

> If Christ has not been raised, your faith is futile and you are still in your sins. Then those also who have died in Christ have perished. If for this life only we have hoped in Christ, we are of all people most to be pitied.
>
> But in fact Christ has been raised from the dead, the first fruits of those who have died. For since death came through a human being, the resurrection of the dead has also come through a human being; for as all die in Adam, so all will be made alive in Christ. (1 Cor. 15:17-22, NRSV)

> "Death is swallowed up in victory."
> "O death, where is thy victory?
> O death, where is thy sting?"
>
> (1 Cor. 15:54-55)

Thanks be to God, who gives us the victory through our Lord Jesus Christ. (1 Cor. 15:57)

God, who made our cosmos in the first place, is a God of life. And so he has "abolished death and brought life and immortality to light through the gospel" (2 Tim. 1:10).

The Scriptures, having set forth so clearly the effect of human sin on the whole cosmos, do not really spell out every detail about nature's processes in God's final kingdom. We are left those questions like, "Will the food chain, by which animals eat one another and gain their sustenance, still be in effect in the kingdom?" Apparently such questions are irrelevant, and we must be content in this life to know in part, until we finally fully know in the kingdom of God as we are already known by our Lord (1 Cor. 13:12).

But this we do know: that if we trust God's work in Jesus Christ, in God's new age nothing will ever again separate us from his love (Rom. 8:38-39), and we shall always be with our Lord (1 Thess. 4:17). Indeed, we will have been transformed into the creatures we were meant from the first to be, reflecting his image (1 John 3:2; cf. 2 Cor. 3:18).

Although the Old Testament writers did not know the resurrection of Christ, they had a glimpse of God's coming victory over death because they participated in a fellowship with God that they finally knew neither death nor anything in life could destroy:

> I am continually with thee;
> thou dost hold my right hand.
> Thou dost guide me with thy counsel,
> and afterward thou wilt receive me to glory.
> Whom have I in heaven but thee?
> And there is nothing upon earth that I desire
> besides thee.
> My flesh and my heart may fail,
> but God is the strength of my heart and my
> portion for ever.
> (Ps. 73:23-26; cf. Job 19:25-27; Isa. 26:19)

Such is our trust too in God in Christ, as we wait in certain hope for his coming kingdom, in which all things will be made new, and heaven and earth will be "very good" again. As 2 Peter says, since all of these things will come to pass, consider what sort of persons we ought to be in lives of holiness and godliness (3:11), waiting in hope and working according to his will and watching with eager expectation for the coming of our Lord. The kingdom of this world will in fact become the kingdom of our Lord and of his Christ (Rev. 11:15). Even so, come, Lord Jesus! Yea, quickly come!

Sample Sermon

I preached this sermon on a first Sunday in Advent at Third Presbyterian Church in Richmond, Virginia. It deals with the second coming of Christ "to judge the living and the dead," and it answers some questions, not dealt with in Chapter 7, about the time of the end and the nature of the judgment.

The Last Phrase

Scripture Lessons:

Romans 13:11-14

Matthew 24:36-44

In the Apostles' Creed, we tell the story of Jesus. We say, "He was born of the virgin Mary, suffered under Pontius Pilate, was crucified, dead, and buried. He descended into hell. The third day he rose again from the dead. He ascended into heaven and sitteth on the right hand of God the Father Almighty. From thence he shall come to judge the quick and the dead." We tell the story of Jesus because it is on the basis of that story alone that we can say, "I believe."

But this first Sunday in Advent in the church year has always had to do especially with the last phrase in that story of Jesus — that last phrase which says, "he shall come to judge the quick and the dead." On this Sunday, which always comes four weeks before

Christmas, we look in two directions. We not only look back in past history eagerly to remember and celebrate the birth of our Lord as a tiny babe, born in a stable-cave and laid in a manger. We also look forward in history to the time when our Lord will come again to set up his kingdom over all the earth. Advent — coming. We look back and remember his first coming at Bethlehem. We look forward to his second coming as Ruler over all.

Now for some of us it is not at all difficult to believe that Jesus Christ is coming again. My husband and I were in an appliance store not long ago, and when one of the clerks learned that we taught at Union Seminary, he asked us, "Do you think we are in the end time?" He was reacting to the California earthquake, you see. Because Matthew 24, from which we read our New Testament Gospel lesson, says that just before the second coming, there will be "wars and rumors of wars; . . . nation will rise against nation, and kingdom against kingdom, and there will be famines and earthquakes in various places" (vv. 6-7). And so the clerk asked, "Do you think we are in the end time?" He had no difficulty believing that Jesus Christ was going to come again.

But a lot of us do have trouble with that basic statement in the Christian faith because it just seems all too strange and fantastic. It seems unbelievable that on some day at some given time, God is going to bring human history to an end, and this world as we know it will pass away.

We have no trouble at all believing that *human beings* may end the world, however. After all, we live in an atomic age, and we know quite well that some madman may push the button that launches the nuclear missiles. And then you and I and this planet will end up as radioactive, incinerated ashes, floating silently through the empty reaches of space. Oh yes, human beings may bring the world to an end. We know that quite well.

But God? Well, that is a different thought, is it not — that God is bringing the world to an end? You see, according to the Bible, the earth is not something that has always been here. No, it had a definite beginning in time when God, the Alpha and

Omega of all time, said, "Let it be!" — and planet earth came into existence. And the earth and life on the earth as we experience it will not just go on in the natural cycle of birth and life and death, evolving endlessly into new forms. No, there will come a day in the fullness of time when God, the goal of all our living, will say, "Enough! Enough of war and rumors of war. Enough of human injustice and greed. Enough of the sin of humankind. The kingdom! Let it be! Let my kingdom come on earth, even as it is in heaven."

And then, our creed and Scripture tell us, Jesus Christ will come again to judge the living and the dead. We all will stand before the throne of Christ and hear his evaluation of us. The world as we know it had its beginning from God, and it will have its end from him. And so Paul in our Epistle lesson can write to the church in Rome, "Salvation is nearer to us now than when we first believed" (13:11). That is, each day we move one day closer to that time when Jesus Christ, the Son of Man, will return to set up God's kingdom on earth.

Our Gospel lesson further tells us, however, that on that day, our God in Christ is going to make some choices. Two men will be at work, it says, and one will be taken into the kingdom, and one will be left outside. Two women will be preparing a meal, and one will be taken and one will be left. And that is the Scripture's way of saying, you see, that God in the return of his Son is going to make some choices among us — choices as to who will inherit the eternal life of the kingdom, and who will be rejected from it.

We very easily forget that, don't we? We go about our daily routine, as our Gospel lesson says, eating and drinking, marrying and giving in marriage, raising the kids, earning a salary, jogging or doing aerobics, reading, napping, watching TV, one day after the next, and all the while we forget that there is that dimension of eternity to our lives — the question always of how we stand in relation to our God in Jesus Christ.

Our society thinks that is all nonsense, of course, and that how it conducts its life is not important to God. Anything goes in this day and age, and many people think that good ol' God will forgive them, no matter what they do. Of course God forgives, they say; that's his business. But as the apostle Paul writes in another letter, "God is not mocked. For whatsoever persons sow, that they will also reap" (Gal. 6:7; my translation). And you and I, in that final judgment, can have our lives count for absolutely nothing in Christ's eyes. He can judge our ways to have been utterly useless in his purposes. And we can be the ones left outside or, in Jesus' figure of speech, the ones who are finally robbed of their home in the everlasting kingdom. When that last phrase takes place and the end comes, as it surely will, God in Christ will make his choices among us.

Well, I don't know how you feel, but that teaching of Scripture can sometimes scare me to death. To borrow some words from a Negro spiritual, "Sometimes it causes me to tremble — tremble — tremble." To think of standing before Jesus Christ our Lord, who has returned in all his risen glory, and to have him examine every minute of how I have lived my life! The saying is true that "God's eye is on the sparrow, but his eye is on the old buzzard, too." And you and I may secretly suspect that we have been one of the buzzards.

And so we can get the same feeling that one woman had when she was touring a monastery one summer. The group on the tour was shown the tiny bare cells where each monk had his cot. And the woman noticed that one monk had painted an eye on the ceiling of his cell. "What's the meaning of that eye," she asked the monk, "that eye painted there above your bed?" "Oh, that is the watching eye of God," replied the monk, at which the woman shuddered and said, "How terrible!" Yes, it may scare us to death to think that God in Christ watches us daily and, at the end, will come to judge our lives.

To be sure, we all have some good things we have done that we could recount to our Lord on that final day — the gifts of time and talent and money that we have given to the church, the comfort or help we lent to someone in need, the kindnesses shown, the prayers uttered, the care and work poured out for the sake of children and families. But in our secret hearts we also know how flawed our lives have been — how anxious we have been sometimes about what we should eat and what we should put on; how unforgiving we have been toward someone who wronged us or who injured our petty pride; how often we have sought our own welfare and status instead of forgetting ourselves in the service of Christ. And so the thought of that last phrase in history — he shall come again to judge the quick and the dead — yes, that causes us to tremble.

But perhaps the question we should really ask ourselves, good Christians, is Why? Why should we tremble at the thought of standing before the judgment seat of Christ? After all, the one who is coming at the end of time is the one whose birth in Bethlehem we will celebrate in just four short weeks. And a loving God sent his Son into the world precisely for the purpose of saving sinners, did he not?

Christ was not incarnate in our flesh and blood to take up residence with a bunch of pure and spotless saints. No. He was born into a world of governmental injustice and of religious zeal gone sour with self-righteousness. He walked streets that were lined with homeless and poor, with prostitutes and cheating tax collectors. He came into homes where two sisters argued over household duties, and where a mother-in-law was sick. He moved among those who were prejudiced against outsiders and foreigners. He wept with those who had lost a loved one. And everywhere, everywhere he brought with him mercy and forgiveness, healing and transformation and a new beginning.

And so when you meet your Lord on that last day, do you think he will be any less merciful? Do you think Jesus Christ returned to judge the living and the dead will suddenly turn into some ruthless and vindictive magistrate who will tally up the score against us, marking every little hatred, every little pride, every little grasping greediness that we so often carry around in our sinful hearts?

No, dear friends, we will meet the same loving and merciful Master whom we have known all our life long — that one who died and rose again that we might be forgiven all our sins, that blessed Savior who has accompanied us and sustained us and guided us every step along our daily way, and who will never leave us, and from whose love nothing in all creation, not even death itself, will ever be able to separate us.

But as our Scripture lessons say, there are some things we must do if we wish to stand there unafraid on that final day of our history, if we wish to greet with joy that last phrase of all our living. We must be ready, says our Gospel lesson, ready for our Lord when he returns.

Now as you well know, some persons have tried to prepare us for that by telling us that they know precisely when Jesus Christ will come again. We often read about such people in the newspapers. They are usually souls who think there is some sort of secret code in the Bible, and so by all sorts of calculations from the Bible's numbers and histories, they figure out that Christ will return on February 17, say, at 3:00 p.m., or they determine that the kingdom will come when all the planets are lined up in a certain way. And then they persuade other naive souls to believe their theories, and they gather their little group and sell all their possessions, and then they go out to stand on a hilltop somewhere to await the return of the Lord.

What they forget, of course, are Jesus' clear words in our Gospel lesson: "Of that day and hour," he said, "no one knows, not even the angels of heaven, nor the Son, but the Father only" (Matt. 24:36). Even Jesus did not know the time of the end, says the Bible, and if we claim we do know it, we are claiming greater knowledge than Jesus had. And so you see, when that clerk in the appliance store asked us, "Do you think we are in the end time?" we had to tell him that we did not know. No one knows when the kingdom will finally come. It may come a hundred years from now. It may come this afternoon. (I always remind my dentist of that when he is debating whether to replace a filling. "Don't drill unless you have to," I tell him. "The kingdom may come tomorrow, and then the filling will be unnecessary!") None of us knows when the end will finally come.

But one thing we do know according to the promises of God, and that is that the kingdom will be a realm in which God himself will be with us, and he will bend down to wipe every tear from our eyes. The violence we know on our city streets will be turned into harmony. The evil in our world and in our sinful hearts will be replaced with good. Death itself will be conquered forever by our Lord who rose from the grave. And there shall be no mourning there, nor crying, nor pain, for the former things will have passed away. And every knee shall bow to Christ and confess his lordly name. And so be ready for that glad kingdom, Jesus tells us. Be ready to receive it at any time, for it surely comes.

And how can we be ready for it? How can we prepare ourselves? By trust, friends, by trust in our Lord Jesus Christ — trust that does not fear the end because it knows that it is our Father's good pleasure to give us the kingdom; trust that believes that Christ wishes only to save us and to give us joy and abundant life; and above all, trust that responds in willing love and obedience to Christ's love and obedience on the cross.

Good Christians, the Advent season in the church is a time of repentance, a time when we once again prepare our lives to receive our Lord who is coming. And God knows — very literally, God knows — we have much for which to repent. We may not have indulged in the reveling and drunkenness, the debauchery and licentiousness that Paul lists in our Epistle lesson — or perhaps we have. But most of us are much more inclined to have engaged in the quarreling and jealousy and other little sins that Paul also mentions. And now the apostle is telling us in his Word to turn around — to repent, to go in the opposite direction, which is what repentance means. Live lives appropriate to those who have been redeemed by the cross and resurrection of Jesus Christ, he says.

But Paul also knows that we cannot do that by ourselves. We have no power in us to correct ourselves and to make ourselves whole. And so what does the apostle say? Put on Christ, he writes. Put on the Lord Jesus Christ. Trust him so much to transform your life and to make you whole that he becomes as familiar to you as the shirt on your back. Trust him so continually every day to clothe you with his power that his Spirit becomes your Spirit and his love your heart's apparel. Put on Christ, and let his commands given in the Scriptures be the shoes that guide your feet. Let his Word be the gloves that direct your hands in service and in mercy. Let his comfort be the coat that protects you from every wintry blast. Let his promises be the scarf that wraps your whole life round and round. Put on the Lord Jesus Christ, and so be ready for the kingdom that is coming.

For that last phrase in our creed about Jesus is true, good Christians. Christ will come again to judge the quick and the dead. He will return to establish God's righteous rule over all this tortured earth. And if we depend only on Christ and put him on, letting him clothe our lives with his love, we need not fear the end nor the judgment, nor anything else to all eternity. The merciful Christ comes to save us and our world, good Christians. Christ comes to save us. Amen.

Sample Sermon

I preached this sermon on a third Sunday of Advent in Second Presbyterian Church in Richmond. It concerns the breaking in of God's new age in the person of Jesus Christ, and I have included it here because it gives illustrations of how the old and new ages might be characterized in a sermon.

B.C. and A.D.

Scripture Lessons:

Isaiah 35:1-10

Matthew 11:2-15

Christmas is the celebration of the breaking of a totally new age into human history.

We are accustomed to dividing time into various periods, are we not? We talk about the Stone Age or the Bronze Age. We look back to the Middle Ages or to the Age of Renaissance. And we like to think that since the Industrial Age, we have been living in the Atomic Age or the Space Age or perhaps the Silicon Age.

But in the thought of our Scripture lessons, there are really only two important ages in human history, and they are characterized by the ones who rule over them. There is the old age ruled by death and all its powers, and there is the new age ruled by Christ. And Christmas is the celebration of the breaking in of that new age.

If we look at the characteristics of the old age, it is very familiar to us, for you and I have lived in it for a very long time. The old age is like a desert, says the prophet Isaiah in our Old Testament lesson. It is the age of desolation, of thirst, of wandering aimlessly through the wilderness of life. Or, in the words of T. S. Eliot, the old age is a wasteland:

> A heap of broken images, where the sun beats,
> And the dead tree gives no shelter, the cricket no relief,
> And the dry stone no sound of water.[1]

The old age is a time of despair, of no hope in the world — where generation after generation of young men go to war's bloody graves with no good result from their sacrifice; a time when the strong strut ruthlessly through the earth and the weak have no helper; an age when violence rules a city's streets and the dark is a place of terror; an age when hatreds fester in our living rooms and families fall apart. The old age is a time without God, when fulfillment lies only in ourselves; a time when pride drives us to a life of constant competition with our colleagues; a time when there is no ultimate meaning to all that we are doing, and work after all is just a way to make a buck. The ruler of the old age is the specter death, and all through the course of it, he inexorably claims his victims, putting an end to every dream, every joy, every lovely human relationship. Yes, I think we know the old age because you and I are living in it. Scholars sometimes call it B.C.E. — before the common era — but it is all too common in our lives now, is it not? And so our forebears in the faith gave it another title. They said it was *B.C.*, before Christ — before Christmas ever came.

And the glad news of the Christian gospel is that there is also an *A.D.* — *anno domini,* the year of our Lord — the new age of Jesus Christ. And it is the breaking in of that new age which we celebrate at this Christmastime.

1. Eliot, *The Waste Land: The Burial of the Dead,* in *Collected Poems* (New York: Harcourt, Brace & Co., 1934, 1936), pp. 69-70, ll. 22-24.

What are the characteristics of this totally new time? It is, said the prophet Isaiah, peering into God's future, no longer a time of desert, of aimless wandering through the wilderness. No, the new age that God has planned is like a time of well-watered abundance, a time when flowers bloom in the crannies of human lives and bent souls are straightened and given some majesty. It is a time when sorrow and sighing have been done away, and joyful song has broken the stillness. It is a time when the powers of death no longer reign on the earth, and human beings are ransomed from the evil forces that hold them captive — from fear, from sin, from anxiety and weakness, from meaningless wandering through their days.

Indeed, proclaimed the prophet Isaiah, when the new age comes, the eyes of the blind shall be opened and the ears of the deaf unstopped; the lame man shall leap like a deer and the tongue of the dumb sing for joy. Human life, with all its still, sad song of sorrow, will be transformed into praise and joy, into wholeness and health.

And so, says our New Testament lesson, to the blind, Jesus Christ said, "See!"; to the deaf, he commanded, "Hear!"; to the dumb, he gave the power of speech; to the lame man, he gave the power to walk. The new age, the age of A.D., has broken into human history. It has begun to come in the person of Jesus Christ, and that is what we celebrate at Christmastime.

And yet, we are very skeptical when we hear such an announcement, are we not? For we have a hard time seeing any evidence of a new age in our world. The forces of death, of fear, of want and brokenness still seem very much with us, and human lives are not much different than they were in B.C. times. After all, for many people the Christmas season is still the loneliest time of the year.

Not too long ago, a writer in one of our church periodicals expressed our skepticism. "If God is involved in the . . . details of human history," he wrote, "[his] will seems a bit capricious at best, handing out a good here, a little neglect or undeserved suffering over there. . . . Explain why," he challenged us, "my cousin Allan was born with cerebral palsy, never to speak a word in his crippled, paralyzed life, and why a starving child in the Sudan does not have the same privileges my own children enjoy."[2] A new age come into human life? Where do we see it? Yes, we are very, very skeptical about B.C. and A.D.

And John the Baptist, in our New Testament lesson, shared our skepticism. He knew all about the healing miracles Jesus had performed. After all, the stories were circulating through all the Galilean countryside. But John was in prison, about to be beheaded by a Roman, Herod Antipas. His country still suffered under the heel of a foreign conqueror. The poor still begged in the streets. The ill still clogged the byways. And John's countrymen still labored and suffered and died under the heat of a desert sun.

And so John sent that delegation of his disciples, you see, to hurl his question at Jesus: "Are you the one who is to come, or shall we look for another?" Are you the one who is going to do away with all this pain of life? Are you the promised Messiah of God who will free us from the Roman yoke? Are you the King who will liberate us from every bondage? John had preached that when the Messiah came — that King sent from God — that King would bring with him fire, burning up the wicked as a farmer burns chaff left from grain.

And so too do we look for some heavenly figure that will rid our world of evil. We fantasize that we will discover life on another planet, and that space-age creatures will come and save us from all our folly. Or, lacking that, we think that we ourselves will bring in the new age of God. By force of arms, we believe, we will rid the world of tyranny. By massive expenditures of federal money, we will conquer want. By education, planning, medical miracles, we will do away with suffering. We are exactly like Jesus said we would be, aren't we? "From the days of John the Baptist until now,"

2. Gordon C. Stewart, "Theology After the Fall," *Presbyterian Outlook*, 3 November 1986.

he said, "the kingdom of heaven has suffered violence, and men of violence [have tried to] take it by force" (Matt. 11:12). By our own wisdom and the strength of our might, we think to bring in the new age.

But to John's challenge — "Are you the one who is to come?" — Jesus answers not a word. Just go and tell John what you see and hear, our Lord replies: "The blind receive their sight and the lame walk, lepers are cleansed and the deaf hear, . . . the dead are raised up, and the poor have good news preached to them" (Matt. 11:5). "How silently, how silently the wondrous gift is giv'n, and God imparts to human hearts the blessings of his heav'n." The new age comes not with cataclysmic conflicts, not in the person of a mighty conqueror on his battle steed, not with fire and shouting and thunder of cannon and drum, but quietly, through the faithfulness of a peasant woman in a stable, giving birth to a helpless infant who grows up in a carpenter's shop.

And since that birth in Bethlehem, have we also not had much to tell of what we have seen and heard? Of desolate lives blossoming into abundant wholeness through the work of Christ's Spirit? Of old sins forgiven and cast away so that persons can start all over again? Of food fed to the hungry by Christ's people and relief sent to the suffering by his church? Of comfort and healing given to the ill and hope lent to the dying? Dietrich Bonhoeffer too languished in a tyrant's prison, as did John the Baptist, but Bonhoeffer had seen what John only hoped for, and so from that Nazi cell he wrote, "By good powers, wonderfully hidden, we cheerfully wait, come what may." "Good powers, wonderfully hidden" in a birth at Bethlehem. A new age has broken into our lives at Christmastime.

Is it any wonder, then, that our Lord could tell us that even the least of us is greater than John the Baptist — that last great prophet, that forerunner of the Messiah from God, that messenger who went before his face? You and I and Dietrich Bonhoeffer and every other member of Christ's church are more privileged than John because our eyes have seen what seers and sages have longed to see — the breaking in of the powers of God's kingdom, of God's new age into our world.

Don Shriver, who is a graduate of our seminary here in Richmond and the former president of Union Seminary in New York City, told of a conversation he had with the great Dutch Christian Hans Hoekendijk. Hoekendijk is dead now, but during World War II he saved 250 Dutch Jewish children from extermination at the hands of the Nazis, and to his dying day he bore on his body the marks of his resistance to the Nazi horrors. "As he recounted these things in his quiet way," said Shriver, "I was brought back to the depressing feeling of what it was like to be alive on this planet during World War II. As I rose to go, I said to him, 'You know, Hans, there are some evils in history that one's imagination cannot really grasp or cope with. The only way to cope with such evils is to try to forget them.' Hoekendijk stared out of the window, and with that long look in his eyes, he finally said softly, 'No, that's not right. There is another way: grace and forgiveness.'"[3] "How silently, how silently the wondrous gift is giv'n, and God imparts to human hearts the blessings of his heav'n." A new age has come into our lives in the person of Christ at Christmastime.

You and I can live in that new age, dear friends. We can be inhabitants of A.D. and not of B.C. And all the wondrous powers of Christ's rule can work their way in our lives and hearts. We can be those redeemed by the Lord that Isaiah talks about — ransomed, set free from the clutches of our guilt, our sin, those awful moments we remember when we injured some soul or spurned God's will or turned our backs on what we knew was good. We can be those rid of our fear of the morrow, and cheerfully wait, come what may, knowing that nothing can separate us from the love of God in Christ Jesus our Lord. We can find a way, a Holy Way, as Isaiah says, that is not an aimless wandering through a

3. Donald L. Shriver, Jr., "Some Words for Beginning," *The Union News*, October 1975, p. 3.

desolate life but a companionship, a joyful walk with a guiding Lord who has promised never to leave us. We can know strength in our weakness, joy in our sorrow, peace that only Christ can give, because it is the peace of God that passes understanding and that the world can never take away. We can learn justice and righteousness and mercy and love from a Lord who is their only source, and find those holy powers working in us to minister to our world in his name and by his Spirit. And yes, we can be among those whom Christ will raise from the dead, free of the finality of the grave and now nevermore fearful of it.

A new age breaks into our lives, its good powers wonderfully hidden in the incarnation of God in his Son, born at Bethlehem. Silently, surely, never faltering, those powers work their way in our world. And we can participate in them if we will trust Jesus Christ and rest our lives in him. A.D. has come, good Christian friends. This is the year of our Lord. And if you will, you can celebrate that, with exceeding joy, at this Christmas. Amen.

CHAPTER 8

The Preacher's Opportunity

In preaching about God's relation to the natural world, ministers have a pregnant opportunity to combine the proclamation of the gospel with their teaching ministry from the pulpit. Certainly the teaching ministry needs to be reclaimed. Far too many preachers have turned the educational work of the church over to directors of religious education and the Sunday school, while they themselves have delivered what might be called merely therapeutic and inspirational messages. The result has been widespread ignorance of the content of the Bible, and included in that ignorance has been a lack of understanding of the actual relation of God to the natural world, as that relation is revealed to us through the richly prolific testimonies of the Scriptures.

Preachers must reclaim those scriptural testimonies if they wish their people to grow in their knowledge of God and in Christian maturity, and if they wish their people to understand their real place in this wondrous world that a merciful God has created. By doing so, preachers will not only enrich their parishioners' lives but will also enable their people to assess and correct the ideas, ideologies, and idiocies that barrage them daily in our secular society.

Reviewing Basic Affirmations

I have discussed some of that societal bombardment in this book. I have critiqued it and have set over against it the insights about God and nature given to us through the Word of God. In doing so, I have made a series of affirmations that are basic to the biblical, Christian faith. Let us summarize some of them:

1. God is not identical with or contained in the creation he has made, and therefore he cannot fully be revealed through that creation. This affirmation is probably the main thrust that we have uncovered in the biblical material which we have reviewed, and it contradicts the many solely immanental theologies that are so popular in our time and that have led to idolatry on the part of some. That God is other from his creation and yet works in creation through his Word and Spirit is the basis of Christian hope. At the same time, God's holiness or otherness, proclaimed through the biblical Word, has been the necessary precondition for the development of science and technology.

2. Contrary to the views often expressed from the pulpit, modern science is not the enemy of biblical faith — not if it carries out its task of studying and describing the nature of the created universe and does not attempt to reach metaphysical conclusions and ultimate ethical positions on the basis of that study. Rather, modern science can marvelously illumine the ongoing results of the work of God, as it also can improve the conditions of all life on the basis of those results.

3. The universe is not self-creating or self-sustaining, as posited in our widespread secular worldview, but rather is created and sustained by the love and faithfulness of God, manifested in Jesus Christ, who at the end will fulfill his purpose for his creation. The proper responses toward God, therefore, are those of trust, obedience, and praise.

4. The biblical understanding of God's relation to the world is not responsible for our ecological crisis. According to the Scriptures, the earth is never given to human beings to do with as they

like. Rather, the earth belongs to God, and human beings are his stewards, made in his image and responsible always to God for the care of his creation. The loss of this biblical faith lies at the base of our ecological crisis, as it lies at the base of our indifference toward life and our willingness to destroy all forms of life, including human life.

5. The world now is not as God meant it to be but is corrupted in all its parts by human sin and our attempt to escape our creaturehood. Nature has fallen with our fall. The optimistic attempts in our time, so characteristic of many ideological programs, to create a perfect world and society apart from God are therefore doomed to be undermined by continuing human sin. Only God can save the world because only God can transform us and our world to accord with his will. Our role as Christians, therefore, is to work in obedience to his will in eager anticipation of his kingdom, which will surely come.

All of these five affirmations very much need to be preached from the pulpit in our confused age and society. In response to that need, I have made a twofold effort in this book: first, I have tried to gather together and to discuss for the preacher all of the biblical material pertinent to our subject; second, I have attempted to demonstrate in the sample sermons and meditations some ways in which such biblical material can actually be used in preaching.

I have given no sermon outlines, however, because I do not believe that any preacher should rely on someone else's outline in constructing a sermon. To do so is to avoid digging into and wrestling with the biblical text for one's self, and that digging and that wrestling are absolutely necessary in order to preach biblical sermons. Nevertheless, every chapter of this book sets forth concrete biblical material, which, if studied carefully and meditated on by the preacher in relation to the congregation, will form itself into lively biblical proclamation and teaching.

Using the Material in Other Sermons

1. Illustrating the Nature of God

It also further needs to be said that preachers can educate their congregations about God's nature and his relation to his creation by including brief discussions and illustrations of that nature and relation within the context of sermons dealing primarily with other topics. For example, in a meditation on the surpassing worth of knowing Christ Jesus (Phil. 3:3-16), I included this paragraph:

> "I count everything as loss because of the surpassing worth of knowing Christ Jesus my Lord." And that knowledge of Christ is of more value than anything else in the world, is it not? Think of it! Because of God's act in Jesus Christ, you and I can approach God with confidence and express our thanks to him. And imagine what it would be like if we could not do that — never to be able to look at our children and pray, "Thank you, God, for this wondrous, lovable little girl or boy." Or never to be allowed to thank God for the rest of a night, or for the work of a day, or for the comfort lent us by other believers. A story is told of the novelist Harriet Martineau, who claimed to be an atheist. One glorious spring morning on a walk with a friend, Harriet was exclaiming over the birds singing and the sun shining on the first blossoms of spring. So she cried out in exultation, "Oh, I'm so grateful!" to which her more believing friend replied, "Grateful to whom, my dear?" It is because of God's act in Jesus Christ that we know God and can approach him with our thanks.

The preacher can also use material from God's work in the natural world to illustrate the nature of God, but we must understand that usage properly. As we have seen repeatedly in this book, nature is inadequate to reveal God and can rightly be understood only in the context of God's revelation of himself in the histories of Israel and, supremely, in Jesus Christ. Yet, *once that context is employed,* God's work in the material world can then speak to us of his character. For example, this is an excerpt from a sermon I preached on the Valley of Dry Bones, in Ezekiel 37:1-14, which I paired with John 11:17-44:

> Only God can put flesh back on the dry bones of our lives — that God who knit you together with flesh and sinews in your mother's womb in the first place. Only God can breathe a life-giving Spirit back into our existence — that God who at our beginning breathed the breath of life into our nostrils, and who now sustains the regular pumping of your lungs and heart as you sit here this morning.
>
> Think of the vitality of that God! Because of his act of creation, every square foot of ground and every drop of pond water swarm with invisible life. Mammals, fish, crustaceans populate every ocean, and a million birds decorate every sky. And then think of the power of that God! — who can pack the energy of the sun into a tiny atom or send out a root that bursts through rock; who can sustain a hundred million monarch butterflies on a yearly migration from Canada to Mexico; or yes, who can faithfully cause new flesh to grow over the insignificant cut in your finger.
>
> Is it any wonder that in our New Testament lesson, Mary and Martha could tell the Son of that God, "Lord, if you had been here, my brother would not have died." For where God is, there is life and not death. Where God speaks, dry bones are given flesh.

This is an example of using God's work in the natural world to illustrate the vitality and power of the God whose Son is "the resurrection and the life."

In a similar manner, I used illustrations from the life of nature in the following excerpt from a sermon on Haggai 1:13–2:19, paired with Ephesians 2:10-22 and 3:14-21:

> "Take courage. Work, for I am with you. My Spirit abides among you. Fear not." I wonder if we realize the immensity of the powers

> contained in that promise or have any idea of the potentialities that accompany the presence of God. Haggai says that ours is a God who can shake all nations and cause their treasures to fill his temple with splendor. Imagine! — a God who can shake the very earth on its foundations! But he can, can't he? For after all, his touch ignited the sun, and his fingers scattered the stars like jewels across the heavens. His power lifted up the Rocky Mountains and populated the ocean depths with mighty whales. His faithfulness sustains the round of the seasons, so that we know spring will always come. His wisdom linked all life together, so that all creatures have food and habitat. His patience even carved each one of our fingers with a fingerprint of its own, and his care planned every one of us, each one of us unique.
>
> Can you imagine the limitless powers and potentialities present to us with such a God in our midst? Ephesians says that by the riches of his glory he can strengthen us with might in our inner selves. And indeed he can, good Christian friends, indeed God can.

God's power, faithfulness, wisdom, and patience, manifested in the natural world, are used to support the statement from Ephesians 3:16.

2. Countering Idolatry

We should never hesitate in sermons, however, to criticize those in our time who have misunderstood God's relation to his creation. Given the widespread idolatry inherent in some current immanental theologies, I believe such instruction needs to be given from the pulpit. The following is an excerpt from a sermon I preached on faith, based on John 20:19-30:

> Who can measure up to Christ, dear friends? We ourselves? One misguided female thinks so — that one who spoke at a California seminary not too long ago. "Thou art Goddess. I am Goddess." All women have divinity in them, she cries. You see, we've never

recovered from the primeval sin — that sin of Adam and Eve in the garden, of wanting to be our own deities. And a lot of foolish souls are strutting around these days, claiming to be divine. But if you and I are deities, then where were we when God laid the foundations of the earth and all the morning stars sang together? And where will we be sixty or seventy or even twenty-five years from now? Even now our hair is thinning or starting to turn grey. There is no longer the spring in our knees that we knew at age twenty. Feebleness approaches, dear friends, the loss of sight or hearing or mental quickness, and if we be gods, we are dying gods, and therefore not worthy of the name.

Or, say some, God is that Spirit which speaks to us through all of nature's beauty, or he is that ceaseless energy which propels evolution and which is captured in nature's processes. But if God be nature and nature his body, we would never know he forgives us, would we? And worst of all, he would never demand that we do anything. But God in Christ comes asking our deepest love and our obedience to all his commandments. And while the grass withers and the flowers fade, his Word and love abide forever.

Now, now since the incarnation, God can be defined and known only from his Son, and every other deity we would imagine for ourselves is a poor, dying imitation.

Some such instruction, it seems to me, needs frequently to be given, in order that persons do not make the mistake of identifying God with what he has made.

3. *Reminding of God's Sustaining Care*

Yet, we always want our congregations to know that ours is a contingent universe and that nothing can exist apart from God's faithful care. I have preached whole sermons on this topic (see the sample sermon entitled "Contingency, Chaos, and Christ"), but I have also included the thought in sermons dealing primarily with other subjects. For example, this is a paragraph from an ordination sermon entitled "The Ministry of the Word," which I based on 2 Timothy 1:1-2, 8-14; 3:14–4:8:

> You are being ordained as a minister of the Word of God, and that Word, incarnate in Jesus Christ, can make the difference between life and death for a congregation and for all who come in contact with it. It was by that Word that God created this world and all the universe beyond it, and it is by that Word of unimaginable power that he now sustains the order of nature's round. His Word summons forth the stars at night, and because he is great in power, not one of them is missing. His Word commands the sun to rise and sends his rain on the just and on the unjust. His Word arrays the lilies of the field in a glory exceeding Solomon's. And because his Word commands all nature's grace, we know that not a sparrow falls to earth without his knowledge, and that we need not fear though the earth should change and the mountains shake from human chaos.

God's sustaining care encompasses not only the universe but also each one of our individual lives, and that may be the emphasis that the preacher wants to make in one portion of a sermon. I included the following excerpt in a sermon entitled "On Being Wise in This Generation," which I based on Hosea 11:1-9 and Luke 16:1-13, and which I preached at the historic First Presbyterian Church in Norfolk, Virginia:

> When you were an infant church, Hosea says, God loved you, and through all the years it is he who has taught you how to walk.
>
> And as for you personally, is that not the story of your individual life also, that God has been on the scene since the day that you were born? Indeed, while you were still in your mother's womb, his hands fashioned and made you, planning the person that you would be, giving you your unique voice and personality and fingerprints like none others in the world. Since the day that you came forth into light, his breath has sustained your life, faithfully filling your lungs to inhale, exhale, in that regular

> rhythm of his love. Through your childhood, youth, adulthood, his Spirit has never been absent from you. When you have ascended into some joyous heaven, he has been there; when you have dwelt in hell, he has been with you.[1]

Pursuing the same thought are these words, taken from a sermon I entitled "The Journey — the Choice," based on Deuteronomy 30:15-20 and Matthew 7:13-14:

> It is hard to enter into life. But really it is easy too. Because who can help loving the God who has brought us thus far on our journey? He has been by our side every step along the way. When we were still in our mother's womb, his hands shaped and fashioned us. In the marvelous words of Job, he clothed us with skin and flesh, and knit us together with bones and sinews. Day by day, he has sustained our breath and lavished on us his care — placing us in home and family, surrounding us with a world of wonder. Every morning his mercies are new, every evening his watch over us unfailing. When we walk through some dark valley of the shadow, underneath are his everlasting arms. When we know only joy and bright gaiety, he increases gladness by pouring out the glories of the morning, creating color and bird song and light to aid us in celebration.[2]

I have previously mentioned Wisdom theology, which understands God's act of creation to have established certain orders in his universe by which nature is governed and to which human beings must defer if they wish to live wisely and well. But in using Wisdom theology the preacher must not turn the orders established by God into deistic, automatic governors of the world, divorced from the sustaining action of God. I mention such orders

1. This sermon was published in its entirety in *Best Sermons* 5 (San Francisco: Harper & Row, 1992).

2. This sermon was published in its entirety in my book entitled *Preaching as Theology and Art* (Nashville: Abingdon Press, 1984), which is now out of print. I now hold the copyright.

in the following excerpt from a sermon for New Year's Day entitled "Whence Comes Wisdom," based on Job 28:20-28; 1 Corinthians 1:18-25; and Luke 2:36-40. Yet the sermon goes on to speak of God's guidance of us in his revealed commandments, apart from which we do not know how to walk:

> God has established an order in the universe. Certainly we acknowledge that to be true in the realm of nature. The universe all around us is a breathtaking model of order — we have only to watch *Nova* or a *National Geographic* special on TV to see the truth of that. There are billions of amazing forms of life on earth, each perfect in itself, and yet each linked with the other forms around it, so that all fit together and work as they were meant to work. An ant in an anthill cooperates in a fantastic fashion with its fellow workers. It knows exactly what its duties are — when to add its particular mud to the anthill, when to transfer its assigned egg to another room in the hill, when to block its corridor against some intruder.
>
> But we are not so wise as the ant, are we? Our Creator has given us certain instructions too — not built into our instincts, to be sure, but revealed to us in his Word: "Thou shalt not kill; thou shalt not commit adultery; thou shalt not steal; thou shalt not bear false witness against thy neighbor; thou shalt not covet" — and yet we persist in thinking we can go against that order of life, maintained in the world by our Creator, and still lead a meaningful and satisfying life.[3]

4. *Prompting Faith's Remembrance*

One of the purposes of Christian preaching is to awaken or to reawaken that saving faith in the God and Father of our Lord Jesus Christ which will lead parishioners to trust him totally and obey him completely. And in the Scriptures, faith is often synony-

3. This sermon was published in its entirety in the November-December 1991 issue of *Pulpit Digest*.

mous with remembering. (See the constant equation of sin with forgetfulness in Psalm 106, for example.) When we remember what God has done in both nature and history, our faith and obedience toward him are called forth. I therefore drew on this motif in a sermon entitled "Forgetfulness in the Desert," based on Exodus 32:1-14 and Revelation 3:1-6. Here is an excerpt:

> "Remember what you have received and heard," says our New Testament lesson. Remember that and repent. And so do you remember, good Christians . . . ? Do you remember how some guilt of the past was lifted from your hearts . . . how God comforted you at the graveside of some loved one . . . those moments of joy in fellowship with the loving Father . . . ?
>
> Or perhaps you remember the joy you felt in the beauty God has lavished around you — that autumn night when the stars shone crisp and clear; that garden of daffodils, azaleas, dogwood that overwhelmed you with its color; that spring morning when the grass was fresh with dew and a cardinal sang outside your window.
>
> Or do you remember the gratitude to God you felt for the laughter of your little child, for his sturdy little legs, and his healthy body, and his chubby little arms round your neck?
>
> There is so much to remember about this God of ours and the blessings he has lavished upon us.

5. *Describing Human Nature*

At the same time that the preacher is proclaiming the gospel of grace and illustrating it from the world of nature, the preacher also has the unique opportunity to teach us about our human nature and how we fit into our universe. This is an excerpt from an Ascension Day sermon, based on Luke 24:44-53 and Acts 1:1-11, that stressed the fact that Christians, transformed by the love of Christ, are not just ordinary people anymore:

> The love poured out now in our midst by Christ in his Spirit . . . keeps us from ever being ordinary again. . . . Indeed, maybe it is

> that love which really makes us human. Anthropologist Dr. Richard Leakey tells us that it is not our brains which first separated us in the course of evolution from the animals. No, what truly separated us from our relatives, the chimps and baboons, explains Leakey, was not our intelligence but our generosity. Sharing, not hunting or gathering as such, is what made us human. We are human because our ancestors learned to share their food and their skills in an honored network of obligation. We were made in the image of God, you see, restored in us by the love of Christ. And because that love is poured out on us now, we are not ordinary creatures.[4]

We human beings need to be reminded, however, of the limitations of our knowledge and of our ultimate dependence on that God who is always beyond us and other than we. This is the introduction to a sermon, based on John 14:1-11, that I preached in Harvard University's Memorial Church:

> We stand on the shores of this world's mysteries and gaze longingly out over their depths. For all of our learning and science — indeed, perhaps because of them — we know how much we do not know. For example, what really causes cancer cells to run amok? Or how does the human brain work, and what triggers its impulses? Even our language is an enigma to us — is it necessary for thought? Or what is the human personality, and what happens to it after death?
>
> On every shore of learning the waters of mystery lap at our feet, and out there in the mists dwell the creatures of the strange and unknown. Some ancient mapmakers used to mark the unexplored regions of their world with the phrase "Here be dragons." We could mark the limits of our understanding with the words "Here be mystery."
>
> Biologist Lewis Thomas, who was head of the Sloan-

4. This sermon was published in its entirety in a collection of sermons by women entitled *And Blessed Is She*, ed. Edwina Hunter (San Francisco: Harper & Row, 1990).

> Kettering Institute, once made the marvelous suggestion that we should all agree not to push the atomic bomb button until we have completely understood just one form of life on earth. He then proceeded to demonstrate that we do not fully understand the lowest protozoa. But if Thomas's suggestion were made a universal law and applied to our understanding of ourselves, we would never blow up our world, for beyond all the other mysteries, we do not understand ourselves and our hunger for God. What is it about the human race that has led it in every culture and clime to construct some form of religion?[5]

We human beings also need to be confronted with the results of a totally secular world — that is, of a world from which God is absent. This is an excerpt from the sermon entitled "On Being Wise in This Generation," to which I previously referred:

> We can see the results all around us of trying to live by our own wits in a world without God. We have indeed been very efficient. We have built great cities, but now we cannot eliminate the urban crime that makes us afraid to go out at night, and inner-city slums and chaotic schools send us, fleeing, to the suburbs. We have unlocked the secrets of the atom and gazed at the very heart of nature, but now we have nightmares about a planet slowly dying under a cloud of radioactive dust. We overcame our Victorian prudishness and turned sex into a free and easy game, and now we spend billions fighting genital herpes and AIDS and trying to support the children born to teenage mothers. We have lovely homes and gardens and children, but half of our marriages fall apart. We have extended our lifespan with good nutrition and health care, and now we wonder what to do with senile parents, and whether or not the Social Security system will pay us anything in return.
>
> I sometimes think the story of the novelist Arnold Bennett typifies our age. Rich and renowned, but on his deathbed in his

5. This sermon was published in its entirety in *Preaching as Theology and Art.*

> sumptuous London apartment, he whispered to his mistress as she bent over his dying form, "It's all gone wrong, my dear." Somehow, left to our own devices, in a world devoid of God, everything seems to go wrong, and we leave nothing but bloody fingerprints and scrawled four-letter obscenities on the landscape of the earth. And that would be the worst judgment of all — that God would abandon us to that.

In some such fashion we can teach our congregations about human nature, showing that we never can live wisely and well apart from our relation to our Creator and Sustainer God.

6. *Redirecting Trust*

Congregations also need to be taught, especially in our time of popular immanental theologies, that the world of nature is neither divine nor permanent, and that we therefore cannot rest our hopes for eternity upon some upward, progressive evolution of the world — a world that itself is passing away. I drew on a personal experience to set this forth in a paragraph of a sermon entitled "The Big If," which I took from John 14:15; 15:9-17; and 1 John 5:1-5, and which I preached in Harvard's Memorial Church:

> Where is there anything good that abides and prospers on this sin-pocked planet of ours? I think that question haunted me for a while after the death of my father. My Dad was an avid gardener, and despite the fact that we lived midst the dry and dusty scrub-oak-covered hills of Oklahoma, Dad was determined that we grow up surrounded by beauty. In fact, he promoted gardening and horticulture all over Oklahoma and the Southwest. And so I spent my childhood running and playing in a yard that abounded in iris and roses, where the smell of lilacs and honeysuckle perfumed the air, and brilliant goldfish swam in a lily pond. I could sit under the shade of apple or peach tree or eat strawberries fresh from picking. The colors of hundreds of daylilies greeted me every early summer; towering pin oaks turned scarlet in the

> fall; and in winter, evergreens of every kind were draped with the grace of snow. It was simply an unforgettable gift of good that Dad gave to his children and his city and region. And yet, I visited that garden five years after Dad's death, and I found it bare and ruined — the evergreens brown, the roses gone, the daylilies choked with weeds, and two snarling dogs in a cage over the spot where the goldfish had swum in the lily pond. And I thought, in the words of Gerard Manley Hopkins, "How to keep — is there any . . . latch or catch or key to keep/Back beauty, keep it, beauty, beauty, beauty . . . from vanishing away?"[6]

The sermon then went on to affirm that in God's eternal kingdom, the good we have done and the beauty we have wrought — in Paul's words, whatever is true and honorable, whatever is just and pure, whatever is lovely and gracious — God will use in this world and then bring to completion and keep everlastingly. But that hope is based on God's promised work and not on nature's automatic ways.

The Language of Nature

Finally, the realm of nature furnishes the pulpit with marvelous language. As I said in the first chapter, we preachers rarely use figures and metaphors from the realm of nature anymore because we are divorced from nature's life and are no longer accustomed to thinking in such terms. But that is a deprivation which has terribly weakened our rhetoric, as becomes evident if we compare our speech with that of some of the great preachers of the past, such as Charles Haddon Spurgeon and Paul Scherer.

Sometimes figures from the world of nature can be very simple and yet very accurate in their description of us. For example, in

6. Hopkins, "The Leaden Echo and the Golden Echo," in *Poems and Prose of Gerard Manley Hopkins*, selected and with an introduction and notes by W. H. Gardner (New York: Penguin Books, 1953), p. 52, ll. 1-2.

our sin, are we not very much like poor dumb sheep? We just nibble our way lost and then can't find the way back again.

Or in the lovely little book entitled *Prayers from the Ark,* the rooster portrays us in our strutting pride. "I am your servant, Lord," says the bird, "but don't forget, I make the sun rise."[7] It reminds me of the visit I made once to our county fair, where we strolled through the live poultry exhibit. There were dozens of kinds of roosters exhibited, all crowing and strutting — in their cages. We human beings crow and strut a lot, but we never realize that we are caged and captive to our sin.

Contrarily, there is this expression of humility from George Washington Carver, to whom the South is so indebted for his work with peanut products:

> When I was a young boy, I said to God, "God, tell me the mystery of the universe." But God answered, "That knowledge is reserved for me alone." So I said, "God, tell me the mystery of the peanut," to which God replied, "Well, George, that's more nearly your size." And God told me.[8]

The natural world can also furnish us with very powerful figures of speech. This is the introduction to that sermon based on Ezekiel 37:1-14 and John 11:17-44 which I mentioned earlier in this chapter and which was entitled "The Safari and the Lion":

> Before we go to sleep at night, my husband and I have the habit of listening to some all-news station on the radio — to Philadelphia or New York, Detroit or Chicago, sometimes New Orleans, depending on which station weather conditions will allow us to pick up on any particular night. And as I listen to the reports of crime and drugs and poverty, I sometimes get the feeling that you and I are on a safari trek through the dark continent called

7. Carmen Bernos de Gasztold, *Prayers from the Ark,* translated from the French and with a foreword and epilogue by Rumer Godden (London: Macmillan; New York: St. Martin's Press, 1963), p. 13.

8. Quoted from a sidebar in *The Presbyterian Outlook;* no other source given.

> Time. We are camped for the night on the edge of a jungle; a few flickering campfires are all we have to hold back the darkness. And out there in the night, there prowls around the edges of our camp a lion looking for someone whom he can devour. And the name of that hungry lion in the shadows is Death.
>
> Death prowls always around the edges of our lives, looking for his chance to attack. We dimly sense that, do we not?

The figure of the lion was suggested to me by 1 Peter 5:8: "Your adversary the devil prowls around like a roaring lion, seeking some one to devour." And certainly the Scriptures themselves can furnish us with the most telling images and metaphors and figures of speech from the world of nature. Beyond our own sensitivity to the world around us, beyond our own powers of imagination, beyond any language we may garner from our reading of great literature, the Bible itself gives us hundreds of images from nature with which to enrich our preaching, if only we will study it and let its language seep into our bones.

Moreover, when we rely primarily on the Scripture's own language for the portrayal of God and the natural world, that language will be set in its proper historical context, in which the God revealed to us through Jesus Christ must also be confessed as the Lord of all nature's ways — its Creator, Sustainer, and finally its Redeemer, who will come to make all things new and who will do away with our sin's awful corruption and death in his eternal kingdom of good.

Index of Scripture References

Index of Names